Pathways to Self-Discovery

Tools to Help You Access Your Higher Self
for Guidance & Healing

by
Gina Lake

NUCLEUS Publications
Books for Personal, Family
and Community Well-being

i

Pathways to Self-Discovery
Tools to Help You Access Your Higher Self for
Guidance & Healing
Gina Lake

Cover illustration and book design by Michael McClure

Published by NUCLEUS Publications, Rt. 2 Box 49, Willow Springs, MO 65793. **Send for free catalog**.

Library of Congress Cataloging in Publication Data

Lake, Gina, 1951-
    Pathways to self-discovery: tools to help you access your higher self for guidance & healing / by Gina Lake.
        p. cm.
    Includes bibliographical references.
    ISBN 0-945934-11-4

Printed in the United States of America

DEDICATION

To my mother, who initiated me into positive thinking (and life!) and who has never for a moment wavered in her support of me.

ABOUT THE AUTHOR

Gina Lake is an astrologer and conscious channel with a Masters degree in Counseling Psychology. She resides in Madison, Wisconsin, with her husband, Paul Ditscheit, a transformational facilitator.

ACKNOWLEDGEMENTS

This book is an outgrowth of my own search for understanding and healing. It is for all of you seekers who know in your hearts that life has meaning and that happiness is possible. My deepest gratitude goes to my husband, Paul, for his understanding and support, and especially for his healing presence and dedication to the Light. Without him, I would not have been able to write this book nor would I be exactly who I am today.

Thanks also go to my dear friend Myron Eshowsky for his help with the section on shamanism, and for his love and support. I also would like to acknowledge the members of Jaya, a musical group in Madison, Wisconsin, whose music has inspired my love for God. Blessings to Velga Dunis, Sumner Matteson, Beth Wortzel, and Jim Powell, the members of Jaya, all healers in their own right. Many thanks also to Kay Ortmans for her invaluable help with the section on creative arts and healing. I also want to thank all my friends who supported me—you know who you are! And finally, I am very grateful to Vimala and Michael McClure, my editors, for their insightful suggestions and guidance.

TABLE OF CONTENTS

Influences on behavior—The personality, the ego, and the soul—Holistic defined—Higher states of consciousness and healing—Psychic and esoteric tools for discovering the soul's plan—Psychotherapy's contributions to healing—Emotional illness defined—How to combat negativity and promote emotional health

The relationship between meditation and healing—Meditative therapies—Shamanic healing—Selecting a shamanic healer—Meditation and self-healing

Benefits of past-life regression—Who can benefit—What to expect—The regression—Hypnosis and light trance—An induction—Healing traumatic deaths and violence—Healing phobias—Rescripting—The witness technique—Achieving a higher perspective—Coming out of the regression—Guidelines for selecting a past-life therapist

Creative visualization—Composing and using affirmations—The benefits of relaxation—Progressive relaxation—Trance induction—Visualizations for eliminating blocks—Visualization to counteract feelings of worthlessness—Visualization for perspective—Visualization for embracing challenge—Visualization for weight reduction—Visualization for problem-solving—Visualizations for experiencing your Higher Self—Guided visualization—A journey for obtaining guidance—What to ask on your guided journey

INTRODUCTION

This book is not only about discovering who you are—that is, your unique needs and talents (a worthy enough goal!)—but discovering the Self behind your personal self, who is guiding not only your discovery process but every step of your life. Those seeking to discover themselves invariably stumble upon this higher aspect of themselves in their journey. I believe, in fact, that a desire to know this greater Self is at the base of most people's search. This is not to diminish the importance of the personal self, which is the persona the Self has taken on for the journey we call life. The personal self is a vehicle and a means for learning in this world and, as such, important to understand and master.

Much of the journey of self-discovery entails healing, because we cannot know who we really are or fulfill our potentials until we have cleared away at least some of our emotional baggage. Once healing is accomplished, our greater Self shines through with purity and clarity and we can begin to live from this Self rather than the personal self. Thus, the journey toward self-discovery is a healing journey, a journey toward greater wholeness—toward becoming more of who we really are.

Unfortunately, achieving this greater wholeness can be difficult in a society that does not recognize all parts of ourselves, particularly our spiritual self. This is not so much the fault of society, which does acknowledge spiritual values, but that of science and its view of the human being. Science has spawned psychology, which in turn has spawned psychotherapy, our society's vehicle for emotional healing. Since science only recognizes that which can be measured or perceived by the five senses, Spirit gets left out of the healing equation in our society.

This has created a dilemma in our society and posed a problem for our well-being. If we need help for emotional problems, which we all do from time to time, we have had only psychotherapy to turn to. Besides the fact that psychotherapy is in its infancy, its effectiveness has been marred by its refusal to acknowledge the whole self, including the part of us that is most unmeasurable: our spiritual self.

However, our emotions are intimately tied to our spiritual self. Emotions do not only arise in response to ego needs but to spiritual needs as well. Yes, we get angry when we can't have that new car and we feel ashamed when we have to drive the old one. But feelings are much more than barometers of what our ego wants; they also indicate what our soul wants. Our ego uses feelings to notify us about survival needs, but our soul uses them to notify us about intrinsic needs. Our feelings tell us what we need to feel happy, to feel fulfilled—to feel whole.

Thus, our spiritual self is very much with us in our lives. If science and psychotherapy do not recognize this, then what are they addressing? Without believing in a spiritual self, they are left with defining happiness in terms of ego needs and ego drives.

There is a problem with this. The ego's needs are not always in harmony with the soul's. The ego's domain is survival, and survival for the ego means attaining superiority and getting its own needs met above all. The soul's domain is different. The soul's domain is personal fulfillment, which may even mean sacrificing our needs for a higher cause or for another person. Furthermore, personal fulfillment may require that we delay immediate gratification to achieve a long range goal, something the ego may be unwilling to go along with.

So, the ego and the soul often find themselves at odds. We can find fleeting happiness by fulfilling the ego's goals, but true happiness comes only from alignment with the soul's goals. The ego is, in fact, the servant of the soul, although it doesn't act that way. The ego would have us believe that it reigns—and so would science. That is the problem with psychotherapy, and many people realize this.

Many people today are looking for help that addresses their deepest needs—their soul's needs. They are looking to holistic healers and other alternative practitioners, who understand the relationship between the spiritual self and other aspects of ourselves. And they are looking for ways to heal themselves without turning to professionals. To arm you in your search for greater well-being and happiness, this book will explain some of the methods used by alternative healers as well as describe the principles behind emotional well-being. Many are methods that you can use yourself. In addition, this book will help you determine what you can do on your own and what you might need professional help for. And it will give you guidelines for evaluating and finding professionals who can help you.

Blessings on your journey! May you discover your Self!

CHAPTER 1
The Principles of Emotional Healing

Before you embark on a plan for self-healing or a search for a professional healer, some information about psychology and how the emotions work might be helpful. What will be presented in this chapter goes beyond standard psychology, however. Psychology does not understand all the influences on human behavior. Because of this, most people remain baffled by why people are different from one another. This befuddlement is evident on talk-shows, for instance, which spend hours exploring these differences.

The personality is a mystery if we think of it, as science does, as being shaped solely by our environment, our culture, our parents, and our genes. These influences are not enough to explain our differences. For instance, why does one child in a family become disturbed while another excels and leads a happy life, and why might this happen even with identical twins? Obviously, our theories about why people behave the way they do have some holes in them. One of these holes is not recognizing that we live many lifetimes and that we bring into each lifetime all our previous experiences.

Our scientists also cannot explain why we have unique temperaments. If this could be explained purely by genetics, twins would respond identically from the start; yet we know identical twins can be as different in temperament from each other as any two people. However, once we know about astrology, the mystery of temperament and many other mysteries are solved.

Esoterica recognizes that our personality also is shaped by our past-life experiences, astrological chart, soul's plan, soul age (how many lifetimes we have lived), and other esoteric factors. When added to the more obvious influences, these explain our personality, our behavior, and our attitudes. Even so, our personality is not the totality of our being. It is more like a temporary cloak worn for one lifetime for experiencing life through that costume. One of the differences between most psychotherapists and more alternative ones is a recognition of these other factors and an acknowledgement that we are more than our personality.

Human beings are complex. We have an ego that helps us survive in the world, a personality through which we experience the world, and a soul that facilitates our personality's lessons and tasks during its life on earth. This is the more esoteric, or transpersonal, view of the human being.

Most psychotherapists differ from this view, and their approach to healing therefore differs. Most focus on the ego as the personality's structuring principle and on improving its functioning in the world. Transpersonal psychotherapists, on the other hand, acknowledge the importance of the ego but help the client align to higher needs, to spiritual needs, rather than only ego needs. Jungian analysis, founded by Carl Jung, and Psychosynthesis, founded by Roberto Assagioli, are two well-known transpersonal therapies that pay particular attention to higher needs.

Transpersonal psychotherapies are gaining popularity as people have become dissatisfied with the more traditional and behavioral-based ones. Transpersonal psychotherapies recognize that everyone has a need for meaning and a unique path to tread. Many of them use meditation, imagery, art, music, and movement to help people discover what is meaningful to them. Some brave souls have even ventured to use astrology and other esoteric tools such as the *I Ching* in their practice. Praises to Carl Jung for breaking ground in this area! These techniques as well as past-life regression will be addressed later in their own chapters.

The field of psychotherapy is continually evolving. Transpersonal psychology is the segment of this field that is using methods such as those just mentioned in an effort to make psychotherapy more holistic. "Holistic" refers to methods that consider all aspects of the person and their interdependence. It not only means acknowledging a spiritual self but acknowledging that the spirit, mind, body, and emotions are related. The holistic perspective recognizes that every aspect of ourselves affects every other aspect, and when one aspect is ill, the others also must be addressed.

Certain cutting-edge therapies, described in the next chapter, stretch this definition even further to include an invitation to Spirit to be active in the healing. They recognize that all healing comes from Spirit, and use meditation and altered states of consciousness to access this help. No special training, preparation, or particular spiritual development are necessary to make use of this healing force; it is available to anyone for the asking. You can ask for it in your own meditations or when joined with others in a group meditation. The chapter on meditative therapies describes the process of invoking the healing Light more specifically.

The different aspects of ourselves are often opposed, but they don't have to be. The personality and the ego can be brought in harmony with the soul. When this happens, healing occurs on all levels. It is when the ego takes control of the personality and works at cross purposes to the soul that we experience ill health and unhappiness. Learning to attune to the soul's needs and subordinate the ego to these needs is the key to health and happiness. Learning to shift the locus of our personality from the ego to the soul is the goal of all spiritual paths. Living from soul-consciousness rather than from ego-consciousness brings joy, peace, and health.

The ego will fight to maintain its control, however. It believes its needs and perceptions are supreme, and it wants you to identify with it rather than your true self—your Higher Self. We need to be aware of the many tricks the ego uses to remain in power in our consciousness. It is a tyrant, and not a very wise one. Like an untamed child, the ego rationalizes, cajoles, blames, threatens, scolds, and pleads to get its way. And like a child, the ego must be approached with compassion and love without giving in to its manipulations. Living from soul-consciousness is like being a good parent, being understanding toward the personal self yet firm in upholding what is best for the whole self.

Before we can live from soul-consciousness, we must establish a relationship with our soul, or Higher Self, which requires being willing to listen to it and fulfill its needs. This is where meditation comes in. By stilling our mind through meditation, we are making a clear statement of desire to allow our Higher Self to be more active in our life. We are inviting it into our life and asking for its guidance and healing. This small step greatly advances our spiritual progress and consequently our healing. Spirit is ever-present in our life, but if we have closed down to it, either consciously or unconsciously, it will honor this choice and be less involved. By openly inviting Spirit into our life, we open the floodgates to love and healing and the potential for greater happiness and fulfillment.

Even though the ego likes to believe it is in control and acts as if it is, the soul is really in control and able to create circumstances in which the ego will learn to let go to the soul's wisdom. The soul is at the root of many of the things we cannot change, those things that even our best efforts don't budge. Things that remain hard for us regardless of our efforts may have a higher purpose for being there. We may not be able to know what that purpose is, but acknowledging that one exists is the first step in finding peace. We all have elements in our lives that are uncontrollable and demand surrender.

I mention the need for surrender because it is not emphasized in much of traditional therapy and even in some more holistic approaches. It is common in therapy to try to make people feel good again, when feeling good may not be the most appropriate goal. Sometimes therapy tries to alter conditions that are part of the soul's plan in an attempt to create happiness as defined by the ego. Rather than erasing pain, we need to understand its purpose and allow it to shape us in the way our soul intends. However, accepting pain and allowing it to transform us doesn't mean wallowing in it, feeding it, or identifying with it. Doing this makes living with pain and learning from it especially difficult.

The soul creates a general life plan before birth, and then chooses a moment of birth that will supply the energies necessary for that plan. The astrological chart, which pictures the energies at the moment of birth, describes this plan. Once we are born, we create the specifics of our life through our choices, and the soul releases our lessons into what we have created. Our ego can do little to change our lessons or our plan. Its power lies in being able to choose how it will respond to the plan and what it will do in the future. Our power as individuals rests in this ability to make choices and learn from them. In this sense we do create our life, but always within the framework of our soul's general plan.

Interestingly enough, Dr. Joel Whitton, a professor of psychiatry at the University of Toronto Medical School, has found evidence through his work with past-life regression for the existence of a soul's plan. He was able to regress subjects to the period between lives, which they experienced as light-filled and functioning beyond time and space. His subjects recounted that one of the purposes of this realm was to allow them to plan their next life, including certain lessons they would try to learn. When they were in this realm, "they entered an unusual state of consciousness in which they were acutely self-aware and had a heightened moral and ethical sense. In addition, they no longer possessed the ability to rationalize away any of their faults and misdeeds, and saw themselves with total honesty."[1] This provides some interesting validation to what many of us intuitively feel and to what mystics have told us.

Mystics also view some illnesses and mishaps as one means the soul uses to set people back on track with their plan when they have strayed from it. When we make choices that are out of harmony with our soul's plan, emotional discomfort or illness results, which may manifest as discontent, depression, anger, resentment, despair, apathy, or any number of responses that might send us to a professional for help. These feelings are our soul's way of telling us that its needs are not being met. These feelings can help us find our way back to our soul's plan if we know how to use them for that.

The mental health establishment, centered on the medical model, treats these feelings with prescriptions and analysis, some of which are helpful. But mental health professionals may misinterpret the problem if they don't understand that these feelings are messages about higher needs. Alternative or transpersonal methods recognize this, and try to provide answers using psychic abilities such as channeling, clairsentience, and clairvoyance; and esoteric tools such as astrology, numerology, palmistry, the *Tarot*, the *I Ching*, and the *Runes*. This is one of the important differences between traditional methods of healing and holistic ones.

Let's look at some of these methods employed by alternative healers and transpersonal psychotherapists for understanding the soul's plan, many of which you can use yourself.

Channeling, also know as clairaudience, is the most direct means of receiving information. It is a process by which information is received from nonphysical intelligences. They may be disembodied people awaiting reincarnation or advanced intelligences from other dimensions, including Ascended Masters like St. Germain and Jesus, angelic beings like Archangel Michael, or extraterrestrials.

Information is received in the channel's mind in the form of words, similar to thoughts. If it occurs while the channel is conscious, it is called mental mediumship or, simply, channeling; if it occurs while the channel is unconscious, it is called mediumship or trance channeling. In mediumship, a spirit, or

nonphysical intelligence, temporarily uses the me
to communicate, while the medium has no rememb
communication.

Channeling has its drawbacks, however. The biggest o
that not everyone who channels is in touch with intelligence
who are evolved enough to provide accurate and helpful infor
mation. But even when reliability is not an issue, channeling
can be disempowering. It may foster an unhealthy dependency
on the channel and not give due respect to the person's own
potential for obtaining inner guidance.

Clairsentience is another way of obtaining information. It is
the ability to receive information through a bodily feeling sense.
Those who get information this way also are called empaths,
and for a good reason: They feel what other people are experiencing. They feel, or sense, other people's emotions, physical
pain, and energy fields. If fully developed, a gift like this is very
useful for psychotherapists and others who work with
emotions. When this ability is fully developed, healers can
receive information about the origins of their clients' emotional
problems and how to work with them.

Clairvoyance, the third extrasensory mode, is the ability to
receive information visually. Information is received by clairvoyants through inner imagery in either flashes of disjointed
images, like snapshots, or ongoing movie-like images, which
may be actual representations or symbolic. Clairvoyants are also
able to see the aura and other energies, such as spirits, invisible
to ordinary sight. Although "psychic" and "clairvoyant" are often
used interchangeably, "psychic" actually applies to anyone who
receives information from an extrasensory mode, not just the
visual mode.

Intuition is crucial with all three extrasensory modes. It is
that sense of knowing something without knowing how we
know it. It is beyond reason and usually experienced as a flash
of knowing previous to or detached from conscious thought.
Although intuition operates in everyone's life, it is more developed in some than others (it develops as we evolve) and it
operates more freely in some than others. More will be said
about intuition at the end of Chapter 6.

With both clairvoyance and clairsentience, intuition is needed
to interpret the images or sensations. Initially, with clairvoyance
and clairsentience, pictures and sensations are received without

ιem. As clairvoyance and clair-
he ability to interpret the pictures
ιudience, intuition is crucial in eval-
ormation and its source. Without
eceive false information without
ιese extrasensory abilities is fully
fully developed. So, the degree of
re of the development of one's

r means for obtaining information
about the soul's plan. **Astrology** is the most complex and well-
known of these, and needs no introduction. However, although
most people know what astrology is, few are aware of its depth
and usefulness in healing and spiritual growth. It is capable of
describing the personality, talents, psychological issues and
needs, challenges, spiritual lessons, life task, vocational inclina-
tions, and potential health issues. It also sheds light on the
timing and unfolding of the soul's plan.

Palmistry, more modernly called hand analysis, provides this
information too, with the exception of the life task and specific
timing of events. It is particularly useful for health analysis. This
information is revealed not only in the lines of the hand but by
the whole hand: its flexibility, shape, color, and size; the spread
of the fingers; the length, shape, and thickness of the fingers
and thumbs; its "mounts" (the mounds); and the shape of the
fingertips and nails. Our talents, potentials, genetic inheritance
(including certain character traits), and hence destiny are said to
be revealed by the nondominant hand. How we use that inheritance is revealed by the dominant hand. Thus, palm readers
will compare the hands to see how we are expressing our
potentials.

Some theorize that palmistry works because of the thousands
of nerve endings in the hands. They speculate that the lines in
the hands result from the brain's impulses, which reflect
thoughts, drives, needs, desires, and attitudes and become
imprinted on the hands as lines. These lines change throughout
life—sometimes rapidly—in response to changes in health,
beliefs, and lifestyle. While some lines mark past events, others
reflect current conditions and attitudes and their future ramifications. Thus, past, present, and future possibilities can be read in
the hand.

There is some correlation between astrology and palmistry. The fingers and mounts correspond to certain planets, which have the same characteristics assigned to them as in astrology. The appearance of the fingers and mounts reflects the degree to which the characteristics that correspond to this planet are developed. For instance, an examination of the index finger (the Jupiter finger) will reveal to what degree leadership, confidence, pride, and sociopolitical interests are developed, all characteristics of Jupiter. Each of the four elements of astrology (air, earth, fire, and water), which relate to certain personality types, also corresponds to a particular hand shape.

Numerology is another system, like astrology and palmistry, that is capable of revealing personality traits and the soul's design. It is the science of numbers or vibrations. It holds that everything is made up of vibrations, with everything having its own vibration. The vibration is reflected in the object's or person's name and birth date, which, in turn, can be reduced to a number and interpreted. Numerology also has correlations with astrology: Each number relates to a planet and the characteristics of that planet, although systems vary in their assignment of the planets to the numbers.

Numerology assigns numbers to the letters of the alphabet and adds the letters (numbers) in a name to arrive at a one-digit number that is then interpreted, although some two digit numbers also have interpretations. Each of the numbers from 1-9 has distinct personality traits, both positive and negative, and represents a life path.

The numbers in dates, especially the birth date, also are added together for interpretation. The birth date in particular reveals the life purpose or life path. Even phone numbers and addresses may be added to determine their vibration. Like astrology, numerology is used to ascertain cycles and the most appropriate or fruitful times to act. It does this through an analysis of the birth date. Numerology is especially useful for understanding cycles and the timing of your soul's plan.

The Tarot is a popular divinatory tool used in prediction, choice-making, and obtaining guidance about the soul's plan. However, it does not offer the information about the personality, inherited traits, psychological needs, spiritual lessons, or talents that astrology, palmistry, and numerology do. Its purpose, like all divinatory tools, is to answer questions. It provides a way of communicating with our Higher Self and sheds light on the forces at work in a given situation.

The Tarot is a set of 78 cards, 22 of which are known as the *major arcana* and represent archetypal forces. The remaining 56 cards, or the *minor arcana*, fall into 4 suits that correspond to the four elements (earth, water, air, fire), or the physical, emotional, mental, and spiritual aspects of ourselves. The minor arcana is the forerunner of our deck of playing cards.

After formulating a question and focusing on it, the cards are shuffled and laid out in a certain pattern, called a spread, and then interpreted. Both the placement of the cards in the spread and their relationship to each other as well as the meaning of the cards that come up are used in interpreting the answer. There are many kinds of spreads used, allowing for many different kinds of insights.

The **I Ching,** which means the *Book of Changes,* is both a divinatory tool and a book of ancient Chinese wisdom. It was written by numerous authors over many centuries, beginning as early as the third millennium B.C., and has been venerated in China for thousands of years. It is perhaps the oldest book in the world. Many renowned Chinese philosophers, including Lao Tsu and Confucius, both studied the *I Ching* and influenced it. It is used today, as it has been throughout antiquity, to gain insight into the changing circumstances of life.

The philosophy behind the *I Ching* is that in everything lies the seed of its opposite, and everything in the universe is changing into its opposite. Life is a continual ebb and flow, which manifests in cycles and rhythms both personally and collectively. The *I Ching* helps you tune in to this ebb and flow so that you can align yourself with it.

The basis of both the wisdom and the divination are eight trigrams. A trigram is made up of three parallel broken or unbroken lines. The eight trigrams are archetypes that symbolize the many possible human conditions or situations on earth. When they are paired in every possible way with each other, sixty-four hexagrams are created, which provide guidance about a particular situation.

After formulating a question and becoming centered, the hexagrams are arrived at by throwing three coins six times; yarrow stalks or other objects also may be used instead of coins. Each toss of the coin results in either a broken line or an unbroken one. Six tosses creates a hexagram. The meaning of the resulting hexagram or hexagrams is looked up in the *I Ching* and meditated upon.

The **Runes** are another ancient divinatory tool, also dating back thousands of years. They were last used in Iceland in the late Middle Ages and were resurrected recently by Ralph Blum, the author of *The Book of Runes*. The Runes are archetypal symbols that work like the Tarot and the *I Ching* in helping us connect with our inner guidance. Like the *I Ching*, the Runes are considered an oracle, an entity of great wisdom.

The Runes are 25 small, flat stones made of clay with a glyph engraved on one side. They come in a draw-string pouch and are accompanied by *The Book of Runes*, which explains the meaning of each Rune. Runes also can be handmade of wood or another substance, for the object upon which the symbols are written is unimportant.

To use the Runes, a question is formulated and focused upon. Then, a Rune is chosen from the pouch to signify the answer to the question. Or, several Runes may be chosen from the pouch and laid out in a pattern, or spread, with each position having a certain meaning. For instance, three Runes may be chosen one at a time and laid out from left to right, with the first Rune signifying the overview of the situation, the second Rune signifying the challenge, and the third Rune signifying the course of action called for. *The Book of Runes* is then consulted for the meaning of the Runes that were chosen.

We do not know the origin of astrology, palmistry, numerology, the Tarot, the *I Ching*, or the Runes. They have been used for thousands of years in cultures throughout the world, but there are no records of how they came into being. Knowledge of these tools was preserved in the Egyptian mystery schools and others, and perhaps developed in these esoteric centers of learning. Some speculate that these tools were given to humankind by beings of advanced intelligence.

We also do not know why these esoteric tools work. Synchronicity, as defined by Carl G. Jung, may explain why the Tarot cards, the Runes, the *I Ching*, and other divinatory tools are able to provide satisfying answers to questions. The idea that whatever happens in a moment reflects the essence of that moment may explain how a moment can be read by cards, stones, coins, or other objects tossed at that moment; or how a person's energy can be read by noting the position of the stars at the moment of that person's birth. Many maintain that the cards, stones, or coins fall the way they do because of spiritual forces. Others speculate that the subconscious somehow controls how the cards, stones, or coins fall. In any event, the mechanism of how these tools work is less important than that they work.

Some counselors who use esoteric tools are not psychic but have enough intuitive development to use them successfully. Others barely need these tools, because their intuition or psychic abilities are so developed. They may use these tools only as a guide or as a prop for structuring their session. On the other hand, some counselors are not intuitive and rely almost entirely on the esoteric tool and their knowledge about it, which is likely to result in inaccuracies. Therefore, it is impossible to evaluate the effectiveness of a healer by his or her tools or lack of them. The effectiveness of a healer will always be a function of intuitive development, and the tools or lack of tools is largely a matter of initial training, habit, or preference.

Those working in the healing professions who are not intuitively or psychically developed must rely on training and experience to know how to proceed in the healing process, since esoteric tools will be of little help. Healers who are not intuitive may have difficulty determining whether what a client is experiencing is a reflection of the soul's plan or a digression from it, and most psychotherapists would not even pose this question. Without knowing this, however, it is hard to direct the healing process. Just how is this determined if the healer is not intuitive?

Those in this position usually rely on certain techniques, particularly intellectual analysis and trance work. **Trance work,** which allows messages from the client's unconscious to become conscious, is being used more commonly now by even more traditional psychotherapists, who formerly relied on analysis alone to determine their clients' underlying motives and needs.

The problem with analysis and with some trance work is that these methods do not retrieve information from beyond the unconscious, where the soul's plan is. The soul's plan is not revealed by working with the unconscious but with the superconscious, and trance work does not tap the superconscious mind unless specifically directed to. Trance work, like meditation, stills the mind through focused awareness on something—

music, imagery, a voice, or an object—but only meditation acknowledges a Higher Power and openly asks to experience this Higher Power. Meditation, therefore, is trance work with a spiritual intent.

The work going on in many psychotherapists' offices lacks this spiritual orientation and is therefore limited in being able to retrieve information that would aid healing. Understandably, this is a touchy area for traditional psychotherapy, which prides itself in its scientific and intellectual approach. But psychotherapy limits itself when it considers only the mind, body, and emotions and neglects the spirit. It is like taking a shadow of an object for the object. Our personalities, bodies, and minds are mere shadows of ourselves. Trying to heal the shadow without regard to what creates it makes no sense.

Despite traditional psychotherapy's shortsightedness, it often manages to help people. Even from its limited perspective, it helps people become more comfortable in their personalities and teaches them to use their strengths to overcome their weaknesses. This is no insignificant feat, for we are here to unfold ourselves within our given personality structure. Becoming comfortable within it is one step toward unfolding our potentials and fulfilling our life plan.

Psychotherapy performs another service by teaching people to be aware of and express their feelings. When feelings are acknowledged and accepted, pent up energy that can be used more productively is released and lost parts of the self are reclaimed. Furthermore, once negative feelings are released, they can no longer cause physical problems. Teaching people to communicate their feelings positively also improves their relationships.

Psychotherapy serves an important function for many. The methods that will be explored in the following chapters can be used in addition to psychotherapy to broaden its scope. These methods are in no way contradictory to psychotherapy nor can they necessarily replace it.

From a holistic standpoint, a healer's ability to experience expanded states of consciousness is as crucial to the healing process as his or her ability to receive information about the soul's plan. Expanded states allow healers to act as conduits for the Higher Power. To act in this capacity, they must be able to reach a state in which they are functioning apart from their egos. This can only be achieved through extended daily meditation.

An expanded state of consciousness also enables healers to transcend their personal consciousness and personal issues. This is valuable, because the healing process may falter or take a wrong turn if the healer's own issues become entangled with the client's. Working from a higher state of consciousness, ensures that no abuse of power will occur either wittingly or unwittingly. It also ensures that the client receives whatever healing is needed and appropriate.

Shifts in consciousness in the client also are crucial to the healing process. They come about in several ways. Sometimes, just receiving meaningful information obtained intuitively or psychically is enough to move someone into a deeper awareness of the Self. For example, uncovering information about an incident in a past life may be enough to free the blocked energy related to it and shift that person's consciousness. In other instances, a shift in consciousness occurs because of the soul's energy work, which removes blocks in the aura. And finally, a shift in consciousness may occur in response to the healer's ability to act as a conduit for a higher vibration of energy. This is sometimes called spiritual healing.

Spiritual healing, or laying on of hands, when performed by someone skilled in transmitting energy, can remove blockages in the energy field that are preventing the person from being comfortable with his or her personality and from a clear experience of the Self. The blockage will recur, however, unless the underlying reason for it is understood and healed. So, maintaining a healing brought about by a laying on of hands may be difficult if other methods are not used to heal the underlying cause of the block.

Complete healing requires a multifaceted approach, including psychotherapy, transpersonal insight, and energy work. Psychotherapy helps people change their behavior and attitudes, which decreases the possibility of blockages in the aura recurring. Transpersonal insight through astrology, channeling, the Tarot, psychic awareness, or other means supports change by offering spiritual understanding and a reason for change. Or, transpersonal insight may simply help people live in peace with what cannot be changed. Energy work frees blockages in the aura so that the old patterns that are being eliminated are not reinforced in the energy field. By working at the problem from all three angles, the potential for long-term healing is greatly increased.

This brings us to the issue of whether or not every physical and emotional difficulty can be healed. When physical illness is solely a product of imbalance, poor habits, or other choices and unrelated to another lesson, it may be healed by the appropriate treatment. But sometimes physical illness cannot be healed, because the illness is providing an important lesson. When this is the case, the illness will subside only when the lesson is learned. So, physical illness can result from poor choices or from the soul's plan or both.

Emotional illness is different, however. Emotional illness is something we create by unhealthy thoughts and feelings. It is not created by our souls for our growth. Therefore, unlike some physical illness, the soul never stands in the way of emotional healing. In fact, calling on the soul to provide emotional healing is an important step in being healed.

Emotional illness can be avoided by learning ways of managing our feelings and by unlearning patterns that create negative emotions. It is not that we can erase negative emotions once they arise; we should acknowledge and accept them if they exist. However, we can learn not to create them by becoming aware of our thoughts, feelings, and needs and by taking steps to manage them before a negative emotional state results. This process is aided by observing our thoughts and feelings as they arise, and by learning to identify with the Self that exists beyond our personal self—our Higher Self. It is usually not possible to accomplish this degree of detachment, however, without a regular practice of meditation. Nevertheless, awareness of our thoughts and feelings can be learned in psychotherapy or sometimes on our own.

It might be helpful to define emotional illness and describe its effect on our energy field. Emotional illness is a state of emotional disease or discomfort with ourselves. It may be the result of guilt, sadness, shame, anger, self-pity, hatred, depression, jealousy, or rage. These negative emotions and the thoughts that create them cause irregularities in the energy field, or aura, which may coalesce into blockages and even manifest as physical illness. Once a blockage forms, it reinforces the emotion responsible for it. Thus, a vicious cycle is created between the negative emotion and the blockage. Just eliminating the negative emotion or the blockage is not enough to break this cycle. The cycle can be temporarily broken by eliminating both. However, the negative emotion will eventually recreate the blockage unless the thought pattern behind it is corrected.

Because thoughts are behind negative emotions and auric irregularities, correcting our thoughts can correct auric irregularities. However, this is not always easy, because the reasons for these thought patterns are complex. Although thoughts seem to arise from nowhere, their origin is often the unconscious, a mysterious and mostly uncharted aspect of ourselves.

It is now recognized that memories stored in the unconscious affect our thoughts and behavior. The significance of early childhood experiences has been particularly well documented. Less recognized, however, is that memories from our former lives, also stored in the unconscious, have a similar effect. Acknowledging the importance of past-life memories will be the next frontier in emotional healing. This will be the first step in releasing their power over us.

Information from the superconscious about our soul's plan also is stored in the unconscious, and also affects our thoughts and behavior. The superconscious, or that part of us that directly experiences God, delivers information and motivations into the unconscious that will help us accomplish our lessons and life plan. Once in the unconscious, they are intuited by us. The astrological chart and other esoteric factors also work this way to create drives that help us with our lessons and life plan. These drives are released from the superconscious into the unconscious and from there to the conscious mind where they manifest, in part, as our personality.

There are a number of ways of working with the unconscious to eliminate negative messages from these various sources, as you will see in the following chapters. There also are many things we can do on a conscious level to combat negative thoughts. One is to become aware of our thoughts by observing them as they arise. By observing them, we put ourselves outside them—in relationship to them—rather than inside them and identified with them. This step is crucial in gaining mastery over them. Once we learn to witness our thoughts, we can choose to follow them, dismiss them, or replace them with others.

Usually, replacing thoughts is easier than dismissing them, which is where affirmations come in. An **affirmation** is a positive statement that counteracts or contradicts a negative thought. It affirms what you want to be true, not what you fear or what you believe you lack: *I give thanks for a healthy, vital, strong body; I am comfortable with my femininity/masculinity; my sexuality is a beautiful part of me; there is enough of everything to go around; everyday I grow more patient; prosperity is mine;* and *I am filled with love for all of humankind* are a few examples.

Even if we are not convinced of what we are affirming, replacing a negative thought with a positive affirmation helps eliminate the pattern of thinking negatively. Initially, it may be necessary to pretend to believe these positive thoughts until a habit of thinking positively becomes established. After a while, the negative thought loses its power and the positive thought begins to feel true.

One problem with affirmations is that some people think they will bring them anything they want. This is magical thinking. Unfortunately, our lives are not created by our wishes, but by our choices, our actions, other people's choices, and the interweaving of these choices and actions with our soul's plan. Although affirmations serve a purpose, particularly in eliminating negative thought patterns that block our happiness and potential, they alone will not solve our problems. Affirmations are merely part of a process that leads to healing and a healthy way of life. More will be said about affirmations in Chapter 4.

Another way to combat negativity is to live in the present rather than in past hurts or future fears. Living in our memories of the past and our projections of the future keeps us from being fully in the present, where joy is ever available. This tendency to live in the past or the future instead of in the present is a mental habit that can be broken with awareness and willingness. Once we realize the importance to our well-being of living in the present, we are better able to discipline our mind to do this.

Meditation is especially helpful in bringing us into the present and the joy available there. Meditation is focused awareness on what is, whether it be on a sensation, an ideal, a sound, or an image. In meditation, we focus our entire attention until we become immersed in whatever we are attending to. This immersion is living in the presence of that object, ideal, sound, or image. At that point, no past or future exists, only the present moment.

Practicing meditation regularly establishes a habit of being in the present. The more we meditate, the more easily we can maintain this state of consciousness, for being in the present is a state of consciousness: a consciousness of pure joy. So, a regular practice of meditation is key in attaining greater peace and harmony in our life and in our emotions.

Another thing we can do to eliminate negativity and enhance our emotional health is to act on the needs that arise within us. Much of the mental and emotional illness we see today stems from people's failure to identify their needs and take steps to satisfy them. When this natural process is inhibited, the energy field becomes blocked. These blockages can be seen or felt by those who can sense the aura. Often they can be identified in the body's musculature as well, as body therapies can attest to.

Emotional health also depends on serving others. We need a balanced flow between caring for ourselves and caring for others. We all need to serve; in doing this, we serve ourselves. So, one key to remaining healthy or regaining our health is giving of ourselves to others. People who give out of genuine compassion and a desire to fulfill a need experience a vibrancy and fulfillment that is an inspiration to us all. Although we may think we have to be healed before we can give to others this way, many discover that in losing themselves in others, they are healed.

Emotional health also depends on speaking our truth. This doesn't mean speaking out about everything at every possible chance, but offering our unique perspective when it serves a purpose. Holding back or hiding our truth from others is innately unhealthy. If we are not honest about how we feel and who we are, we risk not living our life plan, which could result in emotional or physical illness or both.

Accepting what we cannot change is another principle of healthy living. We all have challenges presented to us by our soul for growth that are beyond our power to change. Often, these challenges are the very things that bring us new under-standing and move us into states of consciousness that could not have been attained any other way. Keeping this in mind can help us through the rough spots.

Pain is part of life. This fact of life is not proof of a cruel or apathetic God. We willingly venture into existence on the physical plane to experience this reality and its unique laws and lessons, of which pain is a part. As long as we remain in the physical body, growth will include pain. Even when we don't understand the higher purpose for our pain, we have to trust that one exists and keep striving for the best outcome.

Pain does have a purpose. Besides helping us learn our lessons, it helps us move beyond personal boundaries to an experience of our Higher Self. By losing what we are attached to—loved ones, physical functioning, beauty, health, youth, or wealth—we are reminded that what lives on is eternal. We are reminded that we are much more than our personality, our emotions, our posessions, our mind, or our body. Losing the things we believe represent ourselves can bring us closer to realizing our True Self.

This is apparent to those working with the dying, who often witness this spiritual transformation in the eyes of those for whom they are caring. As the ego dissolves, as it often does in lingering terminal illnesses such as AIDS and cancer, the spirit is able to express itself more purely through that person. How important it is, then, to allow people to die in a way that allows this to happen. All who experience this are enriched as well. The dying have much to teach us.

CHAPTER 1 NOTES

1. Michael Talbot, *The Holographic Universe* (New York: Harper Collins, 1991), p. 215.

CHAPTER 1 SOURCES

Blum, Ralph. *The Book of Runes: A Handbook for the Use of an Ancient Oracle.* New York: St. Martin's, 1987.

Cheiro. *Cheiro's Book of Numbers: The Complete Science of Numerology.* New York: Prentice Hall, 1986.

Hipskind, Judith. *Palmistry: the Whole View.* St. Paul: Llewellyn, 1988.

Japikse, Carl. *Exploring the Tarot.* Columbus, Ohio: Ariel Press, 1989.

Javane, Faith and Dusty Bunker. *Numerology and the Divine Triangle.* West Chester, Penn.: Whitford Press, 1979.

Reid, Lori. *The Complete Book of the Hand: A Modern Approach to Hand Analysis.* London: Pan Books, 1991.

Wilhelm, Richard. *The I Ching,* trans. Cary F. Baynes. Princeton, N.J.: Princeton University Press, 1981.

Wing, R.L. *The I Ching Workbook.* Garden City, N.Y.: Doubleday & Co., 1979.

CHAPTER 1 SUGGESTED READING

Handling Feelings

Assagioli, Roberto. *Psychosynthesis.* New York: Hobbs, Dorman & Co., 1965.

Gendlin, Eugene T., Ph.D. *Focusing.* New York: Bantam Books, 1988.

Griscom, Chris. *The Healing of Emotion: Awakening the Fearless Self.* New York: Simon & Schuster, 1988.

Keyes, Ken, Jr. *Handbook to Higher Consciousness.* Berkeley, Calif.: The Living Love Center, 1974.

Viscott, David, M.D. *The Language of Feelings.* New York: Pocket Books, 1977.

CHAPTER 2

Meditation, Meditative Therapies & Shamanism

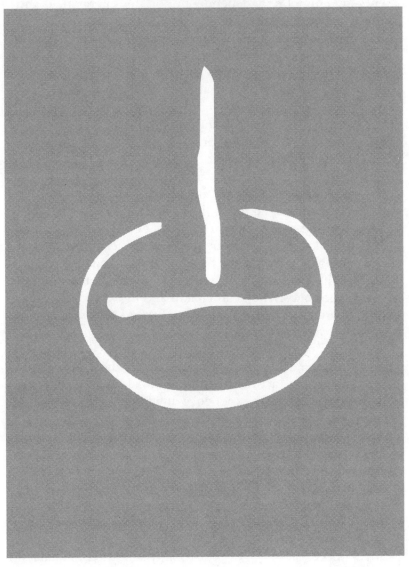

We are not just physical beings; we are energy beings. Our physical bodies are surrounded, interpenetrated, and nourished by an energy field known as the aura. Within the aura are seven swirling vortices called *chakras*, which means "wheels" in Sanskrit. The chakras are connected to the endocrine glands and major nerve plexuses and take in energy for the physical body. Each chakra plays a specific role in our physical, emotional, mental, and spiritual well-being. Our health and well-being are not only dependent upon this energy field and its chakras but reflected in it.

The chakras are aligned along the spine. The first chakra, or root chakra, is located at the base of the spine. Next comes the reproductive chakra, located between the pubic bone and the navel; then the solar plexus chakra, located about an inch above the navel. The fourth chakra, or heart chakra, is located at the heart; and the fifth chakra is at the throat. The sixth chakra is located at the brow or third eye area; and the seventh, or crown chakra, is at the top of the head.

The first three, or lower, chakras are involved with physical, emotional, and mental functioning respectively. The fourth chakra, or heart chakra, forms the bridge between the lower chakras and the higher ones. The *Heart Center*, which includes the heart chakra, is believed by many sensitives to be the seat of the soul, which moderates between the personality, repre- sented by the lower chakras, and the Higher Self, represented by the higher ones. The heart chakra and those above it lie untapped and undeveloped in most of us. As these chakras become activated, great gifts unfold.

All healing comes from the Higher Self, and activating the higher chakras releases its healing power. In those few who have these chakras activated in their normal state, healing is a daily event. They rarely experience anything but balance and harmony in their emotions and bodies. Those of us who don't normally have these chakras activated can activate them through meditation.

Meditation means different things to different people. For our purposes, it will be defined as focused awareness on the breath, an object (such as a candle or a rose), an image (such as a picture of a Master like Jesus), a sound (such as a chant or uplifting music), a word or mantra, a movement, an ideal (such as love, peace, or unity), or one's bodily sensations. Meditation has been known throughout history as the path to spiritual liberation. The reason it raises consciousness so effectively is that it stills the mind, which creates an opportunity for the Higher Self to manifest. Regardless of what we focus on, the result is the same: Our mind and emotions become still and we open a pathway for Spirit to enter our awareness.

What is it about the mind that interferes with God-realization? For one, the mind is the ego's tool unless we make it the Higher Self's. The mind devises rationalizations and logic that keep the ego in power in our consciousness. Furthermore, the mind's busyness blocks communication with the Higher Self.

To commune with the Higher Self, we must go beyond the conscious mind into the domain of the Higher Self, where flashes of intuition can be received. Only once the mind and its chatter are stilled can the Higher Self's voice—or intuition—be heard. As long as we listen to the mind as if it was all that exists, we miss the opportunity to commune with the Higher Self, who is waiting to enter our awareness.

In stilling the mind, meditation also stills the body and the emotions. It lowers the blood pressure; slows the heart rate, metabolism, and respiration; relaxes the muscles and blood vessels; and brings feelings of peace. Herbert Benson, M.D. of Harvard Medical School calls what happens in meditation "the relaxation response" and has found that it is conducive to physical health and emotional well-being. Some researchers postulate that meditation and altered states of consciousness enable messages of healing to be communicated more easily from our minds to our bodies. [1]

Just as yogis are able to control their blood pressure, body temperature, and heart rate through meditation, we are discovering that even ordinary people can obtain extraordinary healing from meditation, a positive mind set, and visualization; and their combination is especially powerful. Dr. Bernie S. Siegel, the controversial surgeon and author, and a pioneer of the mind/body connection claims that there is an actual cause and effect relationship between thoughts and feelings, and physical illness:

There is now a growing body of evidence that the mind and body, the brain and the immune system, are not separate but bound together. We now know, for example, that certain substances produced by the brain transform thoughts and emotions into chemicals, and that these chemicals, in turn, affect the body—either positively or negatively. In short, feelings are chemical and can kill or cure. [2]

In his work with cancer patients, Dr. Siegel has repeatedly observed how positive emotions—ones present in meditation, such as hope, love, peace, unity, and joy—are promoting and sometimes resulting in physical healing.

Herbert Benson, M.D., a cardiologist, would include faith in this list. In his book *Beyond the Relaxation Response*, he discusses how just believing in a healing power within or beyond ourselves is enough to promote healing. He calls this the "Faith Factor", but physicians are familiar with this as the placebo effect. What is original about Dr. Benson's work is that he proved that belief, when coupled with the relaxation response, or meditation, and appropriate medical care can improve a number of physical conditions, including back pain, high blood pressure, headaches, panic attacks, and insomnia.

Thus, making a conscious request for healing to our Higher Self (or whatever you wish to call it) will help us receive the fullest benefit of the Higher Self's healing power, because it affirms our belief in the existence of an outside (or inside) healing agent. Besides, the Higher Self will not transgress our will if we have either conscious or unconscious resistance to being healed; therefore, such a statement helps us align our will to our Higher Self's.

This is why prayer is so important to healing. In prayer we offer ourselves (the ego) up to our Higher Power; we proclaim: *I am open to higher help and I believe it is possible to receive it.* This receptivity and faith is key to healing: We must knock before the door will be opened. Therapies that employ this understanding are greatly enhanced. We also can benefit by making this statement in our own meditations.

As simple as this sounds, this is the hardest step for some. Although most people don't have difficulty acknowledging the existence of a Higher Power, those who blame God for their misfortunes may have difficulty asking God to heal them. This blame will have to be overcome somehow.

Meditative Therapies

Meditative therapies invoke the Higher Self's healing power, or the Light. This healing power is already at work even without requesting it, but it works more effectively when invoked. These therapies are based on the idea that the soul knows what is most in need of healing and will carry this out when asked.

Many healers have discovered the benefits of invoking the Light and call what they do by different names. Many work independently and have developed their work intuitively. Therefore, it is impossible to name specific meditative therapies. Because my experience is with the work my husband does, what I will be describing comes from my understanding of his work.

Once we are aware of the availability of this healing power, we can invoke the Light in our own meditations and learn to follow its energy work. Most people can perceive the action of the Light subtly within their own bodies once they are aware it exists, and their ability to do this improves with practice.

By requesting healing, we open ourselves up to a remarkable resource that pours forth its bounty on us, affecting not only our emotional health but our spiritual well-being. Actually, these are related, for without emotional healing there can be no spiritual growth. So, emotional healing precedes spiritual development and is integral to it. This is especially important for those on a spiritual path to understand. Meditators who experience unpleasant emotions during their meditations may need a more conscious confrontation with emotional issues, perhaps in psychotherapy or with an alternative health care professional. Those with persistent, deep-seated issues, are better off using meditation as an adjunct to professional help rather than relying solely on it for healing.

The facilitator begins by aligning his or her own energy with Spirit by means of a brief period of meditation. After this, he or she speaks an invocation aloud, inviting the Light to carry out whatever healing is most necessary for that person. This can be stated simply, and preferably by the client as well as the facilitator. The following is an example of an invocation:

*Heavenly Father, Divine Mother, we invoke your healing Light
and loving assistance today. Grant us whatever healing is
needed for the body, mind, emotions, and spirit of (name) in
accordance with the highest good of all. We open our hearts to
your love, our minds to your guidance, and our spirits to your
grace.*

Heartfelt words do have the power to release (or reject) the
healing force. If this were not so, we would always receive
whatever healing was in our highest good (although not necessarily in the form we hoped for). But we don't always receive
what we need, because the soul will not transgress our will
when we consciously or unconsciously choose not to be
helped. Because words are one way we acknowledge our will,
words can release the full power of the Light. By speaking an
invocation thoughtfully and with feeling, either silently or out
loud, we acknowledge our desire to be healed.

The transformational process is based on the knowledge that
we are already perfect wholeness, although we may not be
aware of it. So awareness is the key, and healing is just the
result. What prevents awareness of our perfect wholeness? The
answer is contraction in our personal consciousness, which
appears as blocks in our energy field.

A block may reflect a behavior pattern or attitude from a
former life or the current one that is inhibiting the unfolding of
our potentials. Or, it may be related to aspects of the personal
self in need of attention, acceptance, or forgiveness that are
interfering with our growth or experience of our Higher Self.
These blocks are attended to by acknowledging their existence,
accepting the aspect of the personal self creating the difficulty,
and asking that it be healed.

The personal consciousness consists of the physical body, the
emotional body, the mental body, the ego (which is a combination of these), and the personal will. Most people have varying
levels and types of contraction in their personal consciousness,
which prevents their awareness from going beyond that
contraction. For instance, if you are feeling depression, which is
how contraction might manifest, your awareness tends to focus
on that, and you have difficulty being aware of anything
beyond that. The transformational process involves bringing
awareness to the contraction, thereby allowing awareness to
expand.

It is through what Dr. Eugene Gendlin, the author of *Focusing*, calls the "felt sense" that we are able to become aware of the state of the personal consciousness. The felt sense is a much overlooked sense that is present in everyone. It is not a physical or emotional feeling; rather, it directly senses the energy behind the physical or emotional feeling. It also is not intuition; however, from feeling the felt sense of an emotion, an intuition arises about what is behind the emotion. The felt sense is a direct perception of the energy of a person's consciousness. For example, the facilitator asks himself or herself: Is the client's consciousness shut down or in contraction? If so, what is that about? What underlies that? or Is the client's consciousness uncontracted and open? If so, to where does the opening lead? With the felt sense, the facilitator can discover the answers to these questions.

During a session, the facilitator simply sits with a client and, after a brief invocation, begins to feel the energy of the client's consciousness with the felt sense as it reflects within his or her own body. In the beginning, what usually shows up is contraction. The facilitator feels into the energy of this, which allows it to deepen toward what underlies it.

For example, the contraction might be experienced as an energy of emotional heaviness around the chest and throat. By continuing to feel that energy of emotional heaviness or tightness without trying to make it change, the facilitator may begin to notice a sense of deepening. Focusing on that leads the facilitator to what underlies it. When the contraction is first discovered, there is a shift in energy, which is experienced as a kind of loosening of energy—almost as if it feels relief in being found. As the facilitator feels into the underlying energy, an intuition arises about the nature of the contraction.

It may be discovered, for instance, that the energy is related to the client's relationship with his father. A rawness may be felt on an energy level that seems like it would be painful if touched. An intuition may arise that the client's father was demanding and treated him harshly. The facilitator would then ask the client if this was so. It may be that the client still feels raw deep inside and therefore avoids being touched or engaged. In this way, awareness is brought to deeply repressed parts of the client's consciousness. After stating a brief forgiveness and then asking the client's soul to transform it, a release and shift happen, which culminate in an opening of the client's spiritual heart.

A flow of Light from the Heart Center then fills and envelopes the client, which is readily experienced by the client with his felt sense. Over the next months, the client will probably notice things changing in his life. He is likely to feel more open and more willing to be touched and to let others in. This would be a typical beginning session.

The nature of what underlies the contraction can vary greatly, but the process is always the same. Awareness is brought to the contraction and it is freed. Forgiveness and awareness allow the soul access to the contraction, which results in release followed by an infusion of the soul into the personal consciousness.

As the soul emerges into awareness, the chakras are activated and opened. The potential of the chakras lies dormant in most of us, but as the soul activates them, they begin to serve more fully as avenues of the soul's expression in the world. Then our soul becomes more present in our everyday life. We begin to live life from a greater depth—not run by the vagaries of our personal consciousness, like a ship tossed on the sea, but by our soul at a depth beyond that tumult. Our personal consciousness then becomes a vehicle for the expression of our soul.

The soul is a force. It is a clear and penetrating Light, which outshines any darkness in our personal consciousness if only we, through forgiveness and awareness, allow it to move us toward wholeness. Emerson wrote in his essay *The Over-Soul*: "We live in succession, in division, in parts, in particles. Meantime within man is the soul of the whole; the wise silence; the universal beauty, to which every part and particle is equally related; the eternal ONE." Contraction in our personal consciousness separates us into parts and particles and keeps us unaware of our soul—our wholeness. Awareness allows the soul to triumph. Emerson continues:

All goes to show that the soul in man is not an organ, but animates and exercises all the organs; is not a function, like the power of memory, of calculation, of comparison, but uses these as hands and feet; is not a faculty, but a light; is not the intellect or the will, but the master of the intellect and the will; is the background of our being, in which they lie,—an immensity not possessed and that cannot be possessed. From within or from behind, a light shines through us upon things and makes us aware that we are nothing, but the light is all. . . . All reform aims in some one particular to let the soul have its way through us; in other words, to engage us to obey.

This transformational process, when joined with devotion to God and regular meditation, initiates a movement toward the One. It is an easy, comfortable—even joyful process. It feels perfectly natural, because the soul is not other than us. In fact, our soul is our True Self.

How emotional healing is accomplished by the soul through meditative therapies like this one is a mystery and will remain one. Nevertheless, some principles behind this healing process and other types of healing often referred to as energy work or energy healing can be described, since they are behind all healing:

First, because the aura reflects thoughts, feelings, and behavior, negative thought patterns, negative feelings, and emotional wounds from this life and previous lives can be seen and felt in the aura. They are experienced by sensitives as stagnant energy or knots, or sometimes tears, which inhibit, arrest, or disturb the aura's natural flow. Some clairvoyants even see pictures in the aura that depict the cause or origin of the block. Second, since the aura is made of energy, Light can free these blockages and return the aura to its natural state. This is what the soul does during a healing session when invoked. This is also what many energy workers, or energy therapists, like Barbara Brennan have learned to do. In her book *Hands of Light*, Barbara Brennan gives a detailed description of the aura and how she works with it to bring about healing on all levels.

Shamanic Healing

Shamanic healing is based on an ancient healing tradition that employs trance states to acquire information and guidance, and provide healing on every level: physical, emotional, mental, and spiritual. Traditionally, shamans have used altered states of consciousness for diagnosing and treating illnesses, acquiring power from power animals and guardian spirits, divination, obtaining advice from spirit guides or teachers, meeting with spirits of the dead, and helping the dead cross over. [3] Many people today, disillusioned with psychotherapy, are turning to shamanism for healing and spiritual guidance.

The shamanic world is inherently holistic. It sees all of life as interconnected and part of Spirit. It maintains that emotional and physical illness result from falling out of harmony with ourselves and our interrelatedness with all things. Thus, rather than focusing on symptoms, the shaman seeks to restore this harmony. To do this, shamans journey to nonordinary reality for spiritual guidance and employ a variety of other healing techniques, such as restoring lost power, extraction of spiritual intrusions, and soul retrieval.

The shamanic journey is an integral part of shamanic healing. Its purpose is to obtain information or spiritual guidance. Traditionally, shamans did the journeying for the person in need of help and returned with an answer, and many still do this. However, a goal of much contemporary shamanism, the Harner Method ® Shamanic Counseling in particular, is to teach people how to journey themselves. This eliminates the problem, common to psychotherapy and other forms of counseling, of dependency on an outside authority. In the Harner Method®, the shaman's role is that of a teacher and guide. The shaman teaches the client how to journey and what to expect, and guides the client in formulating the question and processing the answer.

The shamanic journey shares some similarities with guided journeys such as the one described at the end of Chapter 4, but they are essentially different experiences. Both occur in altered states of consciousness and are taken to obtain guidance or information; but unlike a guided journey, the shamanic journey is not guided by the shaman and the experience is considered real. Shamans consider nonordinary reality as real or more real than ordinary reality and contend that actions in nonordinary reality directly affect ordinary reality.

Like the meditative therapies just described, shamanism operates on the premise that, when requested, the spirit world will provide whatever healing and help are appropriate to the person. Requesting help from the spirits through invocation prior to shamanic work is therefore an essential part of this work. In the invocation, the shaman asks Spirit to work through him or her. The shaman's intention to bring healing to the person also acts as an invocation to Spirit.

An altered state of consciousness is another prerequisite to

The Essential Ingredients for Emotional Healing

♥ A heightened state of consciousness in the healer to receive information and facilitate the soul's work.

♥ A heightened state of consciousness in the client to enhance receptivity to information and healing.

♥ Invoking the soul to carry out whatever healing is needed.

♥ Making unconscious material conscious.

♥ Engaging the conscious mind and the will in the healing process through awareness and statements of forgiveness.

journeying. It is usually achieved through drumming, which has been found to create theta brain waves in the listeners. In urban settings, a cassette player with headphones and a drumming tape are often used instead of actual drums (in the Harner Method ®). This has the obvious benefit of not creating noise that might disturb others, but it also allows the journeyer to narrate his or her experiences to the shaman as they are occurring, if desired, without the interference of drum noise.

Once an altered state of consciousness is achieved, the shamanic journey can begin. Usually the person journeys to meet his or her power animal, who will provide an answer to the question, often symbolically or through pantomime. A power animal is a spirit guide who takes the form of an animal that has personal meaning to the journeyer. This is likely to be an animal the person already has a sense of connection with, perhaps one he or she happens across more often than most people or one that has had personal significance to him or her, especially in childhood. However, the answer can be received any number of other ways as well. Some possibilities are: through a meeting or conversation with a "mythic personage," a "Great Teacher," a disembodied spirit, or a being from another dimension; through an initiation; or through a visit to another realm. 4

Journeying, especially as it is taught in the Harner Method ®, has many benefits. Besides providing information and guidance, it is a way of becoming acquainted with the spiritual realm and learning how to access spiritual guidance for ourselves. One of the greatest benefits of the Harner Method ® is that once the method is learned, journeying can be done independently. Journeying also provides a place of peace when healing or retreat are needed, something sorely needed in our culture.

Here is one client's account of a shamanic journey, which Myron Eshowsky, a faculty member with the Foundation for Shamanic Studies, was kind enough to share. This client was troubled by rage and chronic depression:

I am going down a tunnel. It is dark and I can only feel the walls as I journey down. I am looking for the end of the tunnel so I can find my power animal. Up ahead, I see the light at the end of the tunnel. I am through now and I notice a very earthy terrain and a forest. I head toward the forest, as I see no animals.

In the forest I see a deer and ask if she is my power animal. She says yes. I ask her how I can get over my rages and not be so depressed. I follow her to a clearing in the woods. There is a large fire in the middle and I see a circle of animals surrounding two people who are fighting. As I look closer, I see it is me fighting me. A chill goes down my spine. The deer tells me they have to work it out. When they start yelling at each other, all the animals make so much noise that you can't even hear them, which startles them out of what they are doing. And when they start to listen to each other and move closer, the animals smile and applaud with their feet on the earth.

The deer goes up to them and tells them they must go into the fire. The angry me goes first. I watch him go up in flame and, as I look into the fire pit, I see a little baby. I reach into the fire and cuddle the baby close to my heart. I feel my heart radiating hot heat throughout my body. The deer tells me to go into the fire with the baby. I feel myself reduced to ashes and then rise in the heat carried by the winds up high to the sky. I feel free at last. Somehow all the ashes settle and I can feel myself going into the soil and then growing back into my original form. The deer tells me it is time to go now. I return to the tunnel and find my way back.

Several weeks later, the client reported that his feelings had remained stabilized and he had none of his former symptoms. He felt he had never been nurtured and that his parents had always kept him from experiencing. He felt the journey had somehow helped him break from this.

Soul retrieval is another shamanic technique, one used primarily for healing. The theory behind soul retrieval is that when people undergo a trauma, such as abuse, rape, combat, incest, loss of a loved one, an accident, miscarriage, abortion, a negative relationship, surgery, or anything that is experienced as traumatic, a part of them leaves—separates from conscious awareness—to protect them from the full impact of the pain. Unfortunately, when this happens some of their vitality, creativity, and joy may leave as well. [5] Soul retrieval attempts to retrieve this lost part of the self and reintegrate it into the personality. Doing this results in a stronger, fuller sense of self and a greater ability to be present in the moment and in the body.

Feelings of being "spaced out," dead, empty, not in our body, detached from feelings, or not being "all there" may be signs of soul loss and the need to regain a part of ourselves. Chronic depression, addictions, memory loss, and physical illness are other possible symptoms of soul loss. [6] These symptoms are the result of the kind of self-alienation traumas often produce.

Like all shamanic work, soul retrieval begins with drumming to induce the necessary state of consciousness. Throughout the soul retrieval ceremony, the shaman lies next to the individual on the floor, while the individual remains relaxed and focused in the present. With the help of power animals, the shaman journeys to wherever the lost part has gone. When the shaman meets this part, the shaman must convince it to return. Once this is accomplished, the shaman "blows" the part back into the individual, and he or she awakens.

Shamanic healing works on all levels and sometimes produces dramatic results. More often, however, its effects are subtle and continue for a long time. Although the individual may not be able to verbalize or even recognize the effects of shamanic work, he or she is likely to feel different and make changes accordingly. What once was acceptable isn't any longer, as the world is approached from a new standpoint—one of greater wholeness. Thus, shamanism is not always credited for these changes; but that is unimportant to the shaman, who approaches the work with an intent to help and the faith that the highest good of all is being served.

Choosing a Shamanic Healer

Today, many are receiving training for shamanic healing through workshops like those offered by the Foundation for Shamanic Studies, founded by Michael Harner. Traditionally, there have been many ways of becoming a shaman. Some inherited the calling and a few even purchased it. But for most, the power was bestowed upon them after surviving a near-death experience or severe illness. Apprenticeship is less common, since most shamans are initiated and taught by spirits in nonordinary reality and therefore don't need an ordinary teacher. [7]

Some contemporary shamans have credentials in counseling and some do not. However, traditional credentials are not an adequate measure of a shamanic healer's potency. In fact, Michael Harner has found that some traditionally trained counselors need to be "deprogrammed" before they can be effective shamanic healers. What is most important, he says, is a "deep understanding" of shamanism. [8]

Perhaps the most reliable and common method for finding a good shaman, since few advertise, is by word of mouth. Miraculous healings are sometimes accomplished through shamans, and when they do occur, word spreads rapidly. Still, there are certain criteria you may want to consider in evaluating a shamanic healer or shamanic healing's potential effectiveness for you (see facing page).

Meditation and Self-Healing

It seems appropriate to end this chapter with a note about meditation and its importance to self-healing. The practice of meditation is essential for anyone serious about healing or spiritual development.

Meditation doesn't have to be ascetic or difficult. It can be

Choosing a Shamanic Healer

★ Interview the shamanic healer either in person or over the phone. What is your sense of him or her? Would you feel comfortable with him or her? A certain match on a personal level is important in any client/ therapist relationship.

★ How does he or she present himself or herself and shamanism? Few shamans call themselves shamans, and good ones never claim they are the one doing the healing. Be wary of anyone who boasts or takes credit for the healing work. Shamans of integrity credit the spiritual realm for their healings.

★ Inquire about training, background, and experience. Training in shamanism is essential. What you don't want is someone who is trying out shamanic techniques after reading a few books, but feels qualified because of other credentials.

★ Questions to ask yourself: Can I visualize? (Fortunately, nearly everyone is able to visualize well enough to benefit from shamanic healing.) Do I want to be helped and am I willing to have things in my life change? Am I open to shamanism? (Shamanic healing can be effective with many issues and ills given the proper attitude and receptivity. Without this, shamanic healing may not be for you regardless of how skilled the shaman is. Even so, shamanic healings do occur without belief or openness.)

done in a comfortable position rather than cross-legged or in a lotus posture, for minutes rather than for hours, and to music or anything else enjoyable. The position, the meditative subject, and the amount of time spent are not as important as regularly setting aside time to do this. Even if just resting quietly apart from the busyness of life each day is all you can do, that is an excellent beginning and serves some of the functions of meditation. If you start simply and make it something you enjoy, your meditations will open up to a richer experience and one you will look forward to.

You don't need to achieve enlightenment to make meditation worthwhile. In fact, the act of trying to achieve anything in meditation is counterproductive to this act of surrender. Moreover, if you are expecting ecstatic experiences and cosmic journeying, you may miss the very subtle and beautiful experience that is offered you. Meditation takes practice and its benefits unfold slowly. You have to patiently attend to the rebirth of the Higher Self into your life.

Attending is an excellent word to describe meditation. Meditation is listening and being receptive to that aspect of ourselves that is greater than the personal self. A daily commitment to meditation is a clear invitation to that Self to become more active in our lives—and that can only bring us greater peace and happiness!

CHAPTER 2 NOTES

1. Bernie S. Siegel, M.D., *"How to Heal Yourself! The Curing Power of Hope, Joy, and Inner Peace,"* Redbook, June 1989, p. 156.

2. Ibid., p. 110.

3. Michael Harner, *"What is a Shaman?" Shaman's Path: Healing, Personal Growth, and Empowerment*, ed. Gary Doore (Boston: Shambhala, 1988), p. 7-8.

4. Michael Harner, *"Shamanic Counseling," Shaman's Path: Healing, Personal Growth, and Empowerment*, ed. Gary Doore (Boston: Shambhala, 1988), p. 180.

5. Sandra Ingerman, *Soul Retrieval: Mending the Fragmented Self* (San Francisco: Harper San Francisco, 1991), p. 11.

6. Ibid., p. 12-14.

7. Michael Harner, *"What is a Shaman?" Shaman's Path: Healing, Personal Growth, and Empowerment*, ed. Gary Doore (Boston: Shambhala, 1988), p. 13-14.

8. Michael Harner, *"Shamanic Counseling," Shaman's Path: Healing, Personal Growth, and Empowerment*, ed. Gary Doore (Boston: Shambhala, 1988), p. 185-186.

CHAPTER 2 SOURCES

Benson, Herbert, M.D. *Beyond the Relaxation Response: How to Harness the Healing Power of Your Personal Beliefs.* New York: Times Books, 1984.

Benson, Herbert, M.D. *The Relaxation Response.* Boston: G.K. Hall, 1976.

Brennan, Barbara Ann. *Hands of Light: A Guide to Healing Through the Human Energy Field.* New York: Bantam Doubleday Dell Publishing Group, 1987.

Harner, Michael. *"What is a Shaman," Shaman's Path: Healing, Personal Growth, and Empowerment,* ed. Gary Doore. Boston: Shambhala, 1988.

Harner, Michael. *"Shamanic Counseling," Shaman's Path: Healing, Personal Growth, and Empowerment,* ed. Gary Doore. Boston: Shambhala, 1988.

Ingerman, Sandra. *Soul Retrieval: Mending the Fragmented Self.* San Francisco: Harper San Francisco, 1991.

Siegel, Bernie S., M.D. *Peace, Love and Healing: Bodymind Communication and the Path to Self-Healing: An Exploration.* New York: Harper & Row, 1989.

CHAPTER 2 SUGGESTED READING

Mind/Body Connection and Healing

Achterberg, Jeanne. *Imagery in Healing: Shamanism and Modern Medicine.* Boston: Shambhala, 1985.

Borysenko, Joan, Ph.D. *Minding the Body, Mending the Mind.* New York: Bantam Books, 1988.

Brennan, Barbara. *Light Emerging.* New York: Bantam Books, 1993.

Chopra, Deepak, M.D. *Quantum Healing: Exploring the Frontiers of Mind/Body Medicine.* New York: Bantam Books, 1989.

Chopra, Deepak, M.D. *Unconditional Life: Discovering the Power to Fulfill Your Dreams.* New York: Bantam Books, 1992.

Dychtwald, Ken. *Bodymind.* New York: Jove Publications, 1978.

Harner, Michael. *The Way of the Shaman*. New York: Harper & Row, 1980.

Locke, Steven, M.D. and Douglas Colligan. *The Healer Within: The New Medicine of Mind and Body*. New York: E.P. Dutton, 1987.

Moyers, Bill. *Healing and the Mind*. New York: Bantam Doubleday Dell Publishing Group, 1993.

Pelletier, Kenneth R. *Mind as Healer, Mind as Slayer*. New York: Bantam Doubleday Dell Publishing Group, 1992.

Siegel, Bernie S., M.D. *Love, Medicine, and Miracles: Lessons Learned About Self-Healing from a Surgeon's Experience with Exceptional Patients*. Boston: G.K. Hall, 1988.

Siegel, Bernie S., M.D. *Peace, Love and Healing: Bodymind Communication and the Path to Self-Healing: An Exploration*. New York: Harper & Row, 1989.

Meditation

Dass, Ram. *Journey of Awakening: A Meditator's Guidebook*. New York: Bantam Books, 1990.

Gunaratana, Henepola, Ven. *Mindfulness in Plain English*. Boston: Wisdom Publications, 1993.

Hanh, Thich Nhat. *The Miracle of Mindfulness: A Manual on Meditation*. Boston: Beacon Press, 1987.

McClure, Vimala. *Some Still Want The Moon* Willow Springs: NUCLEUS Publications, 1989.

Miracles

Markides, Kyriacos C. *The Magus of Strovolos: The Extraordinary World of a Spiritual Healer*. London: Arkana Books, 1990.

Murphet, Howard. *Sai Baba: Man of Miracles*. York Beach, Maine: Samuel Weiser, 1992.

Talbot, Michael. *The Holographic Universe.* New York: Harper Collins, 1991.

Yogananda, Paramahansa. *The Autobiography of a Yogi.* Los Angeles: Self-Realization Fellowship, 1983.

Resources for Transformation and Training in Healing

Barbara Brennan School of Healing
P.O. Box 2005
East Hampton, NY 11937

Energy Mastery Seminars, Inc.
P.O. Box 2339
Sedona, AZ 86336
(founded by Robert T. Jaffe, M.D.)

Esalen Institute
Big Sur, CA 93920

The Foundation for Shamanic Studies
P.O. Box 670
Norwalk, CT 06852
(founded by Michael Harner)

Institute of Transpersonal Psychology
250 Oak Grove Ave.
Menlo Park, CA 94025
(founded by Stanislav and Christina Grof, developers of Holotropic Therapy.)

New York Pathwork Center
61 Fourth Ave.
New York, NY 10003
(the New York branch of Phoenicia Pathwork Center)

Phoenicia Pathwork Center
Box 66
Phoenicia, NY 12464
(founded by Eva Pierrakos)

CHAPTER 3
Past Life Regression

Past-life regression can help us become more whole by freeing us from old emotional, behavioral, and attitudinal patterns that block us. It also can help us get in touch with our greater self—the self that extends beyond this present life, the self that has lived many other lives.

Whether you believe past lives are real or not is not important to benefit from past-life regression. Past-life therapy is effective whether you believe the images are actual images from a past life or just something conjured up by your unconscious. Here is a list of some of the benefits of past-life regression:

Benefits of Past-Life Regression

* It demonstrates that we are more than we appear to be.

* It allows us to experience other personalities, lifestyles, roles, and feelings. This takes us outside ourselves and helps us examine different ways of being. [1]

* It provides an explanation for our behavior, fears, drives, needs, compulsions, or problems. Having justification for these things helps us accept and heal them; the knowledge in itself is healing. It especially helps us understand those responses of ours that are unreasonable, unexplainable, compulsive, inappropriate, and out of proportion to a situation.

* It has been successful in alleviating depression, anxiety, phobias, psychosomatic illnesses, metaphysically-based illnesses, certain skin problems, asthma, gastrointestinal problems, high blood pressure, and headaches. [2] Sometimes dramatic improvement of physical symptoms results.

✳ It brings feelings out into the open where they can be acknowledged, expressed, and accepted.

✳ It gets the unconscious and conscious minds working together toward greater well-being.

✳ It increases creativity and intuition by activating and helping to integrate the right and left hemispheres of the brain.[3]

✳ It is client-centered: The therapist acts only as a guide in the client's healing process.

✳ It requires fewer sessions than conventional therapy, because it quickly identifies the root of the problem.

✳ It can be used to access positive states in past lives. It can help us access personal power, inspiration, and other resources.

Who Can Benefit from a Regression

Past-life regression can be a useful adjunct to psychotherapy, meditative therapies, and other methods of emotional healing. When a painful past-life experience has not been able to be integrated because we are locked into feelings of fear and powerlessness generated by the trauma of that experience, past-life regression can free us from these feelings and help us integrate the experience.

We all have had traumas in our past lives, yet we do not all need past-life regression. Besides the possibility that we may no longer have any traumas lingering in our unconscious, this may be because healing a particular trauma is not on our soul's agenda for this lifetime. What trauma or traumas are chosen to be worked on depends on our other lessons, the karma to be released, and whether working through it fits with the rest of our life plan.

The psychological issue or issues that stem from this trauma (if there is one) can be read in the astrological chart. When a lifetime is to be focused on healing an issue from a former life, the chart may be chosen expressly for this. However, not all past-life issues are significant enough to warrant this. Nevertheless, because every chart will be chosen to address some psychological issue, if not one stemming from a trauma, careful reading of the chart can pinpoint problem areas and indicate a direction for any healing work.

When an entire lifetime is focused on releasing a difficult issue from a former life, this issue may consume most of our energy. Difficult issues like these can shape and distort our perceptions and interfere with our well-being and growth. The overwhelming nature of these issues calls for therapy. Most in this situation are not equipped to work through these issues on their own.

The kinds of issues that present themselves as overwhelming are usually the result of more than one traumatic experience. It is common for someone who has experienced a trauma in one lifetime to try to overcome it in another by facing it again, only to reinforce the fear rather than eradicate it when it is reencountered. This can go on for several lifetimes. When a fear has been reinforced more than once, it can be particularly hard to work through. It may manifest as a phobia or, more commonly, be cloaked in neurotic or compulsive behavior that interferes with one's functioning and happiness.

Whether a psychological issue is caused by a past-life injury or a current one is not always obvious. Many who seem damaged but who have had perfectly normal childhoods and supportive parents may be suffering from pain from a previous lifetime or lifetimes. For them, past-life regression may be in order if the damage is interfering with their functioning. Others who have experienced damage in their childhoods that reinforces past-life injuries and who are making little progress in therapy also may be candidates for past-life regression if the reason for their lack of progress is that conventional means have not been able to reach to the problem's root. Whenever difficulties are particularly resistant to psychotherapy, past-life regression may be in order. Obviously, when psychotherapy is sufficient, past-life work is not necessary.One way to determine whether or not past-life regression is right for you is to consult a channel who can supply information about past lives and what is needed. Channeling is one means by which information of this nature can be obtained. However, care must be taken to find a channel who can reach levels of intelligence (spirit guides) capable of delivering accurate past-life information. Reading past-life records is not easy, and only advanced spirit guides can do this accurately. A good channel also can provide information about other healing options. Some channels even channel regressions themselves, so you may want to look into this possibility.

If you have determined that past-life regression may be helpful to you, here are some criteria for evaluating your readiness for it:

First, you need some familiarity with relaxation techniques or meditation. If you are unable to relax, which will be obvious if you try some visualization exercises like the ones in the next chapter, you will need to practice relaxing through a technique called progressive relaxation; an exercise is presented in the next chapter.

Second, you need some ability to visualize. Are you able to see images during visualization exercises? Not everyone is strong in the visual mode; some people are more auditory and kinesthetic, and will relate better to hearing and feeling than to images. Those who are auditory or kinesthetic can still benefit from past-life regression, but they must have some ability to visualize. This can be developed with the help of the many visualization tapes on the market or by making your own tapes using the visualization exercises presented here or in other books. Learning to visualize will take time, but if you are willing to pursue this, it can be well worth the effort. Visualization exercises, alone, have many benefits, as we will see in the next chapter.

The final criteria is whether you are willing to commit several sessions to past-life regression. It sometimes takes months of weekly sessions to heal and integrate a trauma from a former life. You need to stay with the process until results are achieved.

What to Expect

Before having a regression it is important to know what to expect. If you don't fully understand what to expect, you may back out when the going gets rough, which it often does. Because many of our troublesome behaviors, attitudes, and feelings are means, although ineffective ones, for coping with the fear and other negative feelings created by a trauma in a past life, nearly all regressions will bring us face to face with a traumatic experience. Going back to a traumatic incident and viewing it as if it was happening to someone else helps you integrate it and overcome its negative impact.

In past-life regression, the past incident is not reproduced as the victim experienced it, because this would only reinforce the fear. It is reexperienced from the standpoint of a witness or, in some cases, from the standpoint of the soul. This is an important difference not only in the experience's level of intensity but also in its healing effect. The observer has resources the victim did not have and is able to view the incident objectively, as if it was happening to someone else, as if it was someone else's story. The observer not only learns from this, just as we learn from the characters in a movie, but he or she also is often able to feel compassion for the offender.

This is possible because other elements of the story unknown at the time of the offense are revealed to the observer. If you can gain insight into the aggressor's Higher Self during the regression, you may even experience that soul's response to the harmful act and understand how deeply disturbing it is to that individual's growth. From this higher perspective, you will be able to move from the fearful, powerless position of a victim to a place of understanding, compassion, and forgiveness. So, the shift from victim to observer (or to the soul) empowers you by enabling you to transmute fear into compassion and under-standing—the gifts of the painful experience.

I should add here that I know of past-life therapists who have success allowing their clients to re-experience the feelings of the victim instead of just witnessing the event. Their success can be attributed to their knowing how to work through the feelings that arise in the regression and their commitment to doing this. Any emotions that are re-experienced in the past-life regression must be worked through with the usual therapy methods. The method presented here of keeping the person in the witness role is one way of doing past-life regressions that is safe even for those who are not skilled at working through feelings.

During a past-life regression, images from the past life will emerge from your unconscious as if you were watching a movie; events will just unfold of their own accord as you watch. Feelings will also emerge. You will have a sense of having been there before or of remembering something you once experienced—a sense of *deja vu.* Sometimes there are feelings of nostalgia as you watch the scene unfold. The images can be quite vivid, unlike a daydream.

When the painful incident begins to unfold, you should just watch it without reacting emotionally to it, as if you were sitting in a movie theater, watching an interesting plot unfold. The feelings that will arise are those a moviegoer would experience—excitement, suspense, concern—but they won't be the same as the protagonist's. You will be aware of the feelings of the other characters in the plot in an equally objective way. Moreover, if you ask for it, you will receive insight into what the events mean to the souls of those involved. The therapist will be busy asking you questions to keep you on track and help you uncover the necessary details.

Although the regression will not be a duplication of the initial experience, it may still be uncomfortable at times. Even as an observer, you will feel some of the victim's discomfort, just as anyone watching a disturbing event would. The pain we want to avoid in a past-life regression, however, is the pain that comes from becoming the victim again. This can be difficult to avoid, because the tendency throughout the regression is to return to this role. When this happens, even briefly, the victim's pain will be felt.

The initial session may be only the first step in moving beyond the fear, pain, and anger to forgiveness. It may be necessary to return to this incident several times before you experience it objectively. Each time you return to it, you will come away with more understanding and readiness to forgive. Once you have managed to feel some forgiveness, you are well on your way to healing this experience. You must be patient with this process. It sometimes takes several sessions before an issue is dealt with sufficiently. But with persistence, integration can be achieved.

The fact that past-life therapy may take several sessions before its goal is achieved is not a reflection of its ineffectiveness, but of the strength of the ego, which insists on maintaining its defensive feelings of fear, pain, and anger. The ego is a mechanism of survival, and fear is one of its means of defense. When the ego feels threatened, fear helps it mobilize its other defenses and alert us to future threats. However, when fear is inappropriate or out of proportion to the circumstance, it robs us of energy and prevents us from functioning as fully as we can. Then, it becomes a detriment rather than a help. This is the kind of fear that lingers into the next life after a trauma. It is an automatic, conditioned response which, rather than protecting us, inhibits our functioning.

The only way to eliminate these fears is to go back to the cause, and the only way to do this is through imagery. The unconscious can be asked to make the painful experience available to the conscious mind through imagery. Once the painful experience is made available this way, new resources can be brought to it, making it less overwhelming. This is the theoretical basis for past-life therapy.

THE REGRESSION

Hypnosis and Light Trance

A past-life regression can be performed in an ordinary state of consciousness, a light trance state, or a deeper hypnotic state. The deeper the trance, the greater access there is to details, dates, and other specifics; but these are not always important to the healing process. Usually a light trance is sufficient, although many—in particular those who use the Netherton Technique—have success working with people who are neither hypnotized nor in a light trance.

One of the reasons for working with people in either a non-hypnotic or light trance state is the resistance and fear many have about hypnosis. Perhaps its would be useful to dispel some of the myths about hypnosis:

Facts About Hypnosis

♦ It is not dangerous.

♦ You do not lose consciousness during hypnosis. Hypnosis is a deeply relaxed state, a state of heightened awareness.

♦ You can't be made to do anything against your will.

♦ Hypnosis is not a truth serum; people sometimes lie or make up things under hypnosis. [4]

During hypnosis, we feel a sense of deep relaxation in which we have no desire to move, a sense of detachment from our surroundings, a heaviness and numbness in the limbs, and a sensation of floating. [5]

The method of past-life regression presented in this chapter uses a light trance state. There is nothing mysterious or paranormal about this state. We experience it while driving, watching television, and doing other repetitive activities that require little conscious attention. Anyone who can experience a light trance state can have a successful regression, given proper preparation.

An Induction

Here is an example of an induction for a past-life regression, which induces a light trance state and sets the stage for the regression. It is presented to give you an idea of what an induction is like. It is not suggested that you try to use this alone to induce a regression. You will need someone with experience to guide you:

Breathe deeply and slowly, and relax into a comfortable position in your chair. Feel the softness of the chair beneath you, and feel yourself sinking deeply into its softness. All you have to do is relax and listen to my words.

We're going to take a journey back in time to a place you once knew. It will be like visiting a familiar place, but you will have the sense that you are watching yourself in this familiar place instead of being that individual. There may be times when you find yourself becoming that individual, but try to just observe that individual. It will be like watching a story unfold, except that you are at the center of the story. This story has already happened and is over and done with. But by paying close attention to the details of this story, you may discover something that will help you.

As the story unfolds, remember that we can stop or change the action anytime if we need to. You won't have to experience painful feelings. We will stop or change the action before you feel anything painful. You are in total control of this experience.

Let's begin by boarding the train that will take you back in time to this faintly familiar place. As you board the train, you know that each step is a step closer to your destination. When you arrive in the train's compartment, you look around for just the right seat. Slowly and deliberately you walk toward this seat and sit down. From here, you can see the countryside outside the window.

As soon as you are seated, the train begins to move: slowly at first, and then gradually picking up speed. You gaze sleepily out the window and watch as the countryside becomes a blur of colors. The clackety, clackety sound of the train as it moves over the tracks lulls you, and you feel a deep sense of relaxation and calm. The train continues on through the darkness of the night and on into the early morning, when the colors return and the sunshine makes its appearance again.

You are aware that today you will reach your destination. Today you will meet with a long lost aspect of yourself that needs your attention and comfort. You have chosen to take this journey to help this part of yourself. This part has been lost and isolated from your awareness, and soon it will meet you for the first time and be healed.

As we near the station, the train begins to slow down. Slowly the colors begin to take the shape of trees, landscape, houses, and people. As the train slows to a stop, the focus becomes clearer. You rise to disembark. You feel a sense of expectancy and anticipation about what is waiting for you. As you step down from the train, the scene unfolds.

Take all the time you need to allow this scene to unfold. If you allow sufficient time, a story will unfold that will reveal the lost aspect of yourself. This aspect of yourself is eagerly awaiting your recognition. When you have some sense of a scene, tell me about it, so that I can be there too. Don't be afraid to tell me even the smallest detail, because even it may be important.

After the induction, the facilitator draws out the imagery the client is experiencing and reminds the client to just observe. What happens in the past-life regression depends largely on the imagery that arises.

Certain themes emerge repeatedly in past-life regressions. Pursuit is one of the more common ones. A pursuit is often taken to the point of capture and the action stopped before the trauma is inflicted. At this point, the individual would be asked to identify either what the aggressor is thinking and feeling or what the aggressor's Higher Self is experiencing.

Another possibility is that the pursuit is changed into a game and the pursuer into something harmless before or at the point of capture. Usually this technique of rewriting the story, called rescripting, would not be used unless remaining objective was a problem. More will be said about rescripting shortly.

Another option, which can be an especially effective way to reinstate the victim's power, is to rewrite the pursuit, allowing the victim to become the pursuer and the aggressor, the pursued—without the tragic ending. The result can be comical ("Oh, I thought you were someone I knew"), practical ("Here, you dropped your keys"), or friendly ("Aren't you someone I knew from Washington High?"). This neutralizes the fear and puts the victim in charge.

Because powerlessness is a common theme in past-life regressions, rewriting the story to allow the victim to either be in a more powerful position or experience an inner sense of power (by witnessing the action) can be an effective tactic. Feelings of powerlessness and hopelessness lingering from past traumas can be as immobilizing as fear. So, when power-lessness is an issue, role reversal can help. However, rewriting the story this way is usually not sufficient to heal past-life wounds. It generally needs to be followed by replaying the original trauma and observing it.

Healing Traumatic Deaths or Violence

Many pursuits end in death or violence. It may not be neces-sary to reexperience the violence or the death (as an observer, of course) to clear it from the unconscious, but sometimes these moments must be faced and worked through. The facilitator needs to be intuitive and experienced enough to know what is necessary.

In general, if the death or violent act took place quickly, it is less likely to need to be faced than one that was slow and extremely painful, either physically or emotionally. Also, if pain lingers even after having dealt successfully with the pursuit, then the trauma itself will probably need to be reexperienced. If work with the pursuit was sufficient, you will feel relieved and relaxed; you may even laugh.

When viewing a violent or deadly event, it is especially important to just observe it. If you join with the victim, the action should be stopped and restarted. One technique that might be used during a death scene to help you maintain objectivity is to have you speak to the victim during the traumatic experience, much as someone's Higher Self or guardian angel might speak to him or her in a circumstance like this. The facilitator might direct you to do this by saying something like this:

Now, be her (his) guardian angel and talk to her. Tell her how much she is loved. Tell her she will always exist, that no one can destroy her spirit. Tell her that she did all she could and that she can't change what is happening to her now. Tell her that her death is something she must accept, and that her loved ones are waiting for her on the other side. Ask her to forgive the pitiful individual who is doing this to her, who is hurting his (her) own progress by this. Then as the observer, say goodbye to her as she leaves her body and enters another dimension.

Many death experiences don't need to be healed; every lifetime ends in death. When death is part of a natural conclusion to life, we feel no trauma or lack of acceptance. Usually only accidental, sudden, or traumatic deaths create future psychological damage, the extent of which is determined by the attitude at death. Some examples of traumatic incidents that may warrant past-life regression are attacks by people or animals, transportation or machinery accidents, falling or drowning, natural disasters, rapes and other violations of one's person, political or wartime atrocities such as torture and imprisonment, and death on the battlefield.

Whether a death results from these incidents or not, the trauma may leave its mark. Incidents resulting in death are not necessarily more traumatic than those in which we survive. Often the opposite is true. It can be more devastating to survive and live with the memory and results of a trauma than to escape its haunting in death. Nevertheless, the memory of most traumas cannot be escaped even in death, for they live on in our unconscious and are reflected in our psychology in future lives. This may seem unfair, but it is part of life on the physical plane.

A violent act or death will most often be a problem in future lives if a detrimental feeling or belief has become programmed into the unconscious along with it. We usually draw conclusions related to our feelings of powerlessness, shame, guilt, hatred, or fear at the time of the trauma. These feelings and conclusions become connected with another element in the story or with our sense of self and bleed through into the current life.

For example, if a red-haired man was the perpetrator in a former life and feelings of powerlessness and disgust were associated with that experience, each time the former victim encounters a red-haired man, he or she may reexperience those same feelings. Whenever strong negative feelings cannot be explained by circumstances in the current life, their origin may be in a previous lifetime. Or, if we died traumatically as a result of our own poor judgment, we may distrust ourselves without understanding why.

Healing Phobias

Fears about objects, activities, places, or animals also often have their origin in past-life traumas. Sometimes these fears, or phobias, are so great that they keep us from functioning normally around the feared object. Phobias are easily alleviated through past-life regression. Once the fear's origin is pinpointed, it is just a matter of speaking to what is feared in a Gestalt-type dialogue during the regression. The following is an example of this:

Client: "Snake, why did you make me fall off the cliff?"

Snake: "I didn't make you fall. You weren't looking where you were going. I just wanted you out of my territory. You didn't have to back up."

Client: "Where was I supposed to go? There was nowhere else to go."

Snake: "I don't know. I don't think of these things. I act by instinct, and my instinct was to scare you away by striking at you. I'm sorry you had to die, but that's life."

Client: "Well, that's easy for you to say. You didn't die."

Snake: "What more can I say? These things happen."

Client: "Yes, I suppose they do. I guess you're not so bad. You were just acting instinctively."

Facilitator: "Can you forgive the snake for acting like a snake? Maybe you could tell it that."

Client: "I forgive you for doing what snakes do."

Facilitator: "How does that feel?"

Client: "A little silly, but it feels better . . . reasonable, but I still feel sad."

Facilitator: "Can you forgive yourself for making a mistake that ended your life? Try saying, 'I forgive myself for falling off the cliff.'"

Phobias can sometimes be healed in one session, although further work may still be needed around the sudden or violent death or accident.

Guilt also often becomes associated with a trauma. This is especially true if we witness a traumatic incident and cannot prevent it from happening or if we feel responsible for it. When guilt is connected to something about the scene, compulsions may arise from it. Compulsive washing, for instance, is often an attempt to cleanse unconscious feelings of guilt associated with a past-life trauma. Or, the compulsive act may be related to the actual scene that produced the guilt, as in the case of a man who paced back and forth compulsively, because this is what he did along the edge of the fault line where he watched an earthquake swallow up his family.

Like guilt, shame and feelings of worthlessness resulting from rapes and other similar traumas also become stored in the unconscious if they are not healed. In future lives, these feelings can lead to promiscuity, impotence, fear or shame around sexuality, or further victimization.

Another common theme in past-life regressions is witnessing another's trauma or death. The most traumatic instances are those involving a loved one in which the witness was powerless to help. These situations can be particularly traumatic if the witness was under duress as well—for instance, if he or she also was captured and tortured or forced to watch a loved one suffer. In these instances, remaining an observer may be especially difficult, since that was the stance taken during the tragedy.

Instead, traumas like these can be worked through by having the witness speak to the lost loved one during the regression, and express the sorrow and guilt that did not have a chance to be released. This familiar Gestalt technique, known as the empty chair technique, is effective for both past-life and current loses. It may be all that is needed to work through painful experiences like these. In these cases, as in others, much of the healing occurs just by making what was unconscious conscious.

Sometimes, however, the witness of a tragedy also was involved in its perpetration and continues to be haunted by this. For them, forgiveness is the key to healing. They need to speak to those they have injured, and express how they feel and ask for their forgiveness. Then they need to forgive themselves by stating this out loud. Rewriting the story or just witnessing it is not necessary or appropriate in these situations.

Rescripting

Instead of witnessing an incident as you experienced it in a former life, your past-life therapist may have you rewrite the story while you are reexperiencing it. As the old story is replaced by the new one, fear is replaced by whimsy or some other emotion. Rescripting can provide lightness and humor, which help us go beyond the seriousness of the moment. Humor has a way of distancing us from a painful situation, just as witnessing it does. This is why humor and laughter are healing. If a painful situation can be transformed into something comical, it becomes less personal and poignant. This is what we hope to accomplish in a past-life regression, so that the intensity of feeling created by the initial incident is neutralized and no longer bleeds through into the current life. The following is an example of this technique:

Facilitator: "Now what does she see?"

Client: "I see a man."

Facilitator: "Remember, be an observer: "She sees a man . . ." And what is he doing?"

Client: "He's coming after me! I'm afraid!"

Facilitator: "Now, stop the movie. Just relax and take some slow, deep breaths and listen to my voice a moment. Remember, you are not yourself—you are watching yourself. The girl you are watching is frightened. What can we do to change these feelings? Do you have any suggestions? What would make her feel better?"

Client: "She'd feel better if it was just a game—like tag."

Facilitator: "O.K. Let's see what that would be like. Let's go back to the story where we left it and pretend that they're just playing tag, and tell me how that feels."

Client: "He's running and she's running. She's running fast, but he's still catching up, because she's just a kid. He's going to catch her! I don't like this game!"

Facilitator: "O.K. Let's stop the action again and try something else. What else would take the scariness out of this game?"

Client: "If he were smaller, weaker, or more friendly."

Facilitator: "How do you want to picture him then?"

Client: "Like a playful puppy. I want him to be a little puppy chasing her, wanting her to play."

Facilitator: "All right. Let's go back to the story where we left it and change him into a playful puppy and see what happens."

Here a life-threatening situation has been turned into a game and then a romp with a puppy. This incident will be reprogrammed in the unconscious and stored safely away as a harmless romp with a puppy. The reason this works is that the unconscious operates like a computer. Stating that we no longer want this memory stored as it was is a clear command to this computer, and asking it to replace the bad memory with a good one makes it easier for it to do this.

Rescripting is only used when the witness technique has been unsuccessful, that is, when objectivity and forgiveness have not been achieved. The witness technique is preferable to rescripting, because more insight and understanding can be integrated. Rescripting is useful for neutralizing the painful emotions before trying the witness technique again.

The Witness Technique

The following example illustrates the value of the witness technique:

Facilitator: "What is happening?"

Client: "I'm in a dark alley. Someone is approaching me—a man. He's stumbling around like he's drunk. He doesn't see me yet. I'm trying to get up, but my leg hurts too much and I can't move. He's coming closer. My heart is pounding."

Facilitator: "Stop a moment and remember that you are not this girl—you are just observing her. You see she's frightened and can't move. What does she do?"

Client: "She curls up in a ball, hoping the man won't see her. That's comforting to her, like if she doesn't see him, then he won't see her."

Facilitator: "What happens next?"

Client: "He stops and bends over her and shakes her shoulder to see if she's awake. She's frozen with fear and doesn't move.

He starts laughing and pulls her up to a standing position. Her leg hurts! Then he starts kissing her and grabbing at her clothes!"

Facilitator. "O.K. Stop here. Address the man who is doing this. Address him as yourself, not as the girl. Ask him why he is doing this, as if you were a reporter doing an interview. Remember, this is just a story—someone else's story."

Client. "Why are you doing this, and what are you feeling now?"

Facilitator. "What does he say?"

Client. "He says, 'Who are you? Get outta here! I'm just havin' a little fun.'"
   "Can't you see she's hurt and scared? She doesn't want you to touch her."

Facilitator. "What does he say?"

Client. "He says, 'I wanna see her squirm. It excites me.'"
   "Leave her alone, you brute!"

Facilitator. "That's fine, but don't get personally involved. Respond as if it is only a story with no reality to it. Ask him what he thinks will happen if he carries out his desires. How will he feel?"

Client. "I'm just curious, Sir, how will you feel after you have satisfied yourself?"
   "He says, 'I don't care. It doesn't matter. Nothing matters. Leave me alone.'"

Facilitator. "Let's go back to the girl and see how she is doing."

Client. "Something funny is happening here. The girl isn't so scared anymore. She's beginning to see him as the pathetic character he is. She sees him as weak—not strong—and she's beginning to feel strong inside herself, not physically strong but courageous."

Facilitator: "Do you think you could write another ending to this story now?"

Client: "Yes."

Facilitator: "Let's do that."

If the action had been stopped at the critical point and the aggressor turned into a clown, for instance, the individual would not have had the opportunity to experience the situation from a more courageous perspective. The transformation that took place rewrote the story itself without the need to create a different, more humorous ending. The insight that was gained may seem insignificant from the intellect's standpoint—anyone can see the aggressor is a pathetic character. However, having this realization in a light trance state can be very healing; it reprograms the experience in the client's unconscious. As a result, this memory will no longer evoke feelings of power-lessness, but inner power and strength.

Achieving a Higher Perspective

The perspective of the souls of those involved was not introduced, because it was not necessary. The following takes the same scene and shows how the perspective of the souls of those involved might be used to accomplish the healing:

Facilitator: "What is happening now?"

Client: "He's kissing her and grabbing at her clothes."

Facilitator: "Stop here a moment. Now pretend you are the aggressor's Higher Self, or guardian angel. What is his guardian angel trying to tell him?"

Client: "It's telling him to stop. It's telling him it's wrong to do this."

Facilitator: "Is he listening?"

Client: "No, he doesn't seem to hear."

Facilitator: "What I want you to do is to try to experience his Higher Self, the part of him that knows that what he is doing is wrong. Try to align yourself with his Higher Self. When you feel you have done this, let me know by lifting your right hand. (Pause) All right. What does it feel like to be his Higher Self?"

Client: "It feels peaceful. His Higher Self is loving and understanding toward him. It's trying to help, but it accepts his weakness. It feels compassion for him."

Facilitator: "Continue to see the aggressor from the eyes of his Higher Self. Feel the acceptance and compassion. (Pause) Now become the observer again. What do you see?"

Client: "I see a frightened girl struggling with a cruel, ignorant man."

Facilitator: "Do you feel any different viewing this scene than you did before?"

Client: "I feel . . . softer, gentler about it."

Obviously, the dialogue will not always go this smoothly. It may take several sessions before the Higher Self's perspective is experienced. However, each session will bring this goal closer. Don't underestimate the power of this technique. It is easy to dismiss this work as silly and irrelevant, but it isn't. Working with the unconscious this way can result in healing on deep levels.

Coming Out of the Regression

Being brought out of the regression smoothly and gradually is important. This is usually done through a guided visualization similar to the induction. Here is an example:

Now let's return to our present day reality by boarding the train that brought you here. See yourself getting on the train, step by step, and finding your favorite seat. As you become seated, the train begins to move, first slowly and then picking up speed. Speedily it is returning you to what you know as your current reality. You feel yourself moving quickly through time, forward through time, moving quickly toward your destination in this room. The train is slowing down now, and you are nearly ready to disembark. Taking all the time you need, slowly bring yourself back to this reality and to this room. You can open your eyes whenever you feel ready.

Although the success of a regression is sometimes dramatically apparent during it, other times the result will not be known for a while, since most past-life work continues to have an impact subtly and increasingly for months afterward. To complicate matters, even if changes have occurred, they may be difficult to articulate. If progress is suspected, the issue may be set aside for a month or so, after which it can be reevaluated. However, if there was resistance or a lack of objectivity during the regression, further preparation or past-life work is likely to be needed.

Time does heal. In days gone by, time was often the only healing method available. Fortunately, today we don't need to wait for time to do its healing. There are ways to speed this up. We have psychotherapy to free us from unconscious fears through awareness and verbalization, and we have extrasensory means to provide insight into the causes of our fears and compulsions. But past-life regression can resolve issues from the past even more quickly and effectively than awareness, verbalization, and insight combined. Past-life traumas that would normally take several lifetimes to heal can be healed in less than one lifetime with past-life regression.

Although hypnotic regression is fairly easy to do, not everyone who has learned to regress people has also been trained in working through past-life issues. When searching for a past-life therapist, look for a hypnotherapist or a psychotherapist with training in hypnosis or trance.

Guidelines for Selecting a Past-Life Therapist

♦ What is his/her training and background? Is she/he trained in psychology and counseling? Is she/he trained in hypnotherapy? Where did he/she get this training? What other training does he/she have? How long has he/she been doing past-life regressions?

♦ Are they certified by A.A.P.L.E., A.P.R.T., or A.G.P.L.A.(see below)?

♦ How much past-life therapy do they do in their practice?

♦ Do you feel comfortable with him or her?[6]

To get the names of local past-life therapists, check metaphysical book stores, metaphysical groups, holistic health centers or practitioners, or contact these national organizations:

Association for the Alignment of Past Life Experience
(A.A.P.L.E)
1619 W. Garvey North
West Covina, CA 91790
(founded by Morris Netherton, Ph.D.)

The Association for Past-Life Research and Therapy (A.P.R.T.)
P.O. Box 20151
Riverside, CA 92516

The Atlantic Guild for Past-Life Awareness (A.G.P.L.A.)
P.O. Box 27485
Towson, MD 21285-7485
(founded by Karl Schlotterbeck)

CHAPTER 3 NOTES

1. Raymond A. Moody, Jr., M.D., *Coming Back: A Psychiatrist Explores Past-Life Journeys* (New York: Bantam Books, 1992), p. 113.

2. Ibid., p. 52.

3. Karl Schlotterbeck, *Living Your Past Lives: The Psychology of Past-Life Regression* (New York: Ballantine Books, 1987), p. 216.

4. Raymond A. Moody, Jr., M.D., *Coming Back: A Psychiatrist Explores Past-Life Journeys* (New York: Bantam Books, 1992), p.180-181.

5. Ibid., p. 181-182.

6. Karl Schlotterbeck, *Living Your Past Lives: The Psychology of Past-Life Regression* (New York: Ballantine Books, 1987), p. 314-315.

CHAPTER 3 SOURCES

Moody, Raymond A., M.D. *Coming Back: A Psychiatrist Explores Past-Life Journeys*. New York: Bantam Books, 1992.

Schlotterbeck, Karl. *Living Your Past Lives: The Psychology of Past-Life Regression*. New York: Ballantine Books, 1987.

CHAPTER 3 SUGGESTED READING

Cerminara, Gina. *Many Mansions*. New York: Wm. Morrow & Co., 1950.

Fiore, Edith. *You Have Been Here Before*. New York: Ballantine Books, 1978.

Goldberg, Bruce. *Past Lives Future Lives*. N. Hollywood, Calif: Newcastle, 1982.

Grof, Stanislav. *Realms of the Human Unconscious*. New York: E.P. Dutton & Co., 1976.

Moody, Raymond A., M.D. *Coming Back: A Psychiatrist Explores Past-Life Journeys*. New York: Bantam Books, 1992.

Netherton, Morris and Nancy Shiffrin. *Past Lives Therapy*. New York: Wm. Morrow & Co., 1978.

Schlotterbeck, Karl. *Living Your Past Lives: The Psychology of Past-Life Regression*. New York: Ballantine Books, 1987.

Sutphen, Dick. *Past Lives, Future Loves*. New York: Pocket Books, 1978.

Sutphen, Dick and Lauren Taylor. *Past-Life Therapy in Action*. Malibu, Calif.: Valley of the Sun Publishing, 1983.

Wambach, Helen. *Life Before Life*. New York: Bantam Books, 1979.

Weiss, Brian L., M.D. *Many Lives, Many Masters*. New York: Simon & Schuster, 1988.

CHAPTER 4
Healing with Imagery

Creative Visualization

Creative visualization is the conscious use of the power of imagination to create circumstances in our life or to recreate ourselves. We use our imaginations unconsciously all the time to create our reality, with both positive and negative results: We imagine ourselves tripping, and we trip; we imagine ourselves eating a hot fudge sundae and we go out and get one; we see ourselves as a successful doctor, and we work hard to achieve that; we long for children, and we have them. However, in creative visualization, we harness our power of imagination to consciously create our reality. We become aware of what we are unconsciously creating through our imagination and we consciously choose either to keep creating that or to create something else. This power to create and the responsibility it entails is an awesome one!

Dr. O. Carl Simonton, a radiation oncologist and medical director of the Cancer Counseling and Research Center in Dallas, helps his patients harness the power of their imaginations to combat cancer. He found that certain imagery techniques resulted in a reduction of the negative side effects of radiation, an increase in the length of time people remained alive, and even a cure in some cases among supposedly incurable cancer patients. One example of the kind of imagery he uses is this exercise he designed for a patient named Frank:

> Frank pictured the radiation he received as consisting of millions of tiny bullets of energy bombarding his cells. He also visualized his cancer cells as weaker and more confused than his normal cells, and thus unable to repair the damage they suffered. Then he visualized his body's white blood cells, the soldiers of the immune system, coming in, swarming over the dead and dying cancer cells, and carrying them to his liver and kidneys to be flushed out of his body. [1]

It seems the mind's imagery also can result in illness. In *The Holographic Universe*, Michael Talbot sites examples from Dr. Bernie Siegel's book *Love, Medicine, and Miracles*, which illustrate that how patients describe themselves may relate to the form their illness takes:

> Examples include a mastectomy patient who told him she "needed to get something off her chest"; a patient with multiple myeloma in

his backbone who said he "was always considered spineless"; and a man with carcinoma of the larynx whose father punished him as a child by constantly squeezing his throat and telling him to "shut up!" (p. 86.)

There is no doubt that our minds have a powerful potential for healing, as evidenced also by the placebo effect: Just the belief in a medication often produces a cure. Nevertheless, the concept of creative visualization can be misleading, because it implies that we can create anything by visualizing it. Although everything that manifests is first mentally conceived, not everything that is mentally conceived manifests. Other variables are involved in manifestation. Of primary importance is whether the soul will allow it. If what we want will not interfere with our soul's plan, it may manifest.

Even when our desires are in harmony with our plan, they must be both realistic and acted on before they will manifest. For instance, someone without architectural training cannot expect to get a job as an architect by visualizing one, even if architecture fits that individual's plan. He or she will have to prepare for that career. Of course, there are still other variables, like whether a job exists and whether that individual's style is appreciated by employers. So, both practical and spiritual realities are involved beyond the initial step of visualization.

Creative visualization is especially helpful in getting us beyond our confusion about what we want, which is often what interferes with manifesting it. Having to picture what we want, as we do in creative visualization, forces us to identify it specifically. This is a crucial step. However, this step cannot be successfully taken until we have a clear idea of who we are and of our soul's desires.

Before any attempt at manifesting our desires takes place, this needs to be addressed. If we don't have some sense of who we are and what our soul is seeking to manifest through us, we may manifest something that doesn't fit for us. Ultimately, this is bound to make us unhappy. Much unhappiness can be avoided by making an effort to understand ourselves and our soul's drives before consciously working to create or recreate our life through visualization.

Astrology and other esoteric tools can help us find answers to these questions. By identifying our psychological and spiritual needs, our life task, and our lessons, esoteric tools can help us discriminate between our soul's drives and inappropriate ego-drives. Armed with this information, we are better able to create our lives in keeping with our soul's plan. And, as might be expected, choices that are in keeping with our soul's plan are likely to manifest more easily and successfully than those that are not. Being in accord with our plan helps life run more smoothly.

Once we have determined what we want and sense that it is in keeping with our spiritual plan, creative visualization can clear away any beliefs blocking its manifestation. However, if something other than an attitude or a belief is blocking what we desire, creative visualization may not help. Creative visualization has no power to influence others, although our improved attitude may change their response to us. Creative visualization only opens doors to our desires that we, ourselves, are keeping closed.

Composing and Using Affirmations

Creative visualization and affirmations go hand in hand. A visualization is an image of already having what we desire, and an affirmation is a statement of that and of our worthiness to have it. Like visualizations, affirmations only have the power to dissolve blocks to our desires that we, ourselves, have created. And, like visualizations, affirmations must be in keeping with our soul's plan if they are to manifest.

An affirmation should touch the heart of the problem and evoke an emotional response. It should be in words that fit for you and evoke a sense of "rightness" at a deep level; it should feel good. Therefore, affirmations composed by others, such as those found in books on the subject, are apt to be less powerful than ones that we compose ourselves. The act of composing an affirmation is both a statement of desire to change destructive patterns and of belief in our ability to do this. It also is a way of identifying the problem, an important step in making any change.

When composing an affirmation for yourself, be sure to word it simply. The more simply you word it, the more powerful it is and the easier it will be for you to remember and repeat it. Choose your words carefully; words are powerful! It should be short, simple, and inspiring. Also, write it in the present tense, as if you already have what you want: "I am glowing with vibrant health!" or "I am getting healthier every day" not "I will be healthy soon." And finally, use positive wording: "I speak only kind words" not "I don't say anything unkind."

Once an affirmation is composed, it should be repeated frequently either out loud or silently, especially when the negative thought arises. Singing an affirmation or writing it repeatedly also can be effective. Repeating an affirmation reinforces our desire to change and our belief that we can, and interrupts the negative thought. Since habits become habits by being reinforced, it makes sense that repetition is needed to break them and create new, more positive ones. An affirmation should be repeated until it becomes natural and automatic. Combining it with a visualization will further strengthen it. Above all, believe what you are affirming!

There are two techniques that will strengthen the effectiveness of your affirmations: treasure mapping and clearing. Both are described in detail in Shakti Gawain's book *Creative Visualization*. Treasure mapping is something I first came across through Unity School of Christianity, which emphasizes the Christ within and publishes books on living and thinking positively.

A treasure map is a picture of what you hope to manifest. It could be used to manifest better health, a better relationship, a more fulfilling job, new friends, money, a greater sense of well-being, better grades, a trip, more leisure time, more harmony in the home, or any number of things. There is really no limit to what a treasure map can be used for. Treasure mapping, or the act of making a treasure map, is a way of externalizing and making concrete your image of what you want. The treasure map (some call them image boards) reinforces your goal whenever you look at it or even when you just think about it. It is fortified by affirmations written across it that proclaim your thankfulness for already having what the treasure map represents.

A treasure map is made by drawing, painting, or cutting out magazine pictures to represent what you want. It should picture you as already having attained your goal. Put yourself in the picture, happily enjoying your new state or situation. Somewhere on the map, include your affirmations and the phrase

"This or something better now manifests for me in the highest good of all." (This is a phrase used by Unity School of Christianity.) It is best to keep your treasure map private. This way, its power cannot be dissipated by other people's disbelief, criticism, or negative thoughts.

Keep your treasure map simple. Choose just one area of your life to focus on (your job, health, relationship, friendships, finances, etc.) rather than including pictures of everything in your life you'd like to be different. For instance, from time to time, I've used treasure maps to inspire me to get in shape. I've found that looking at a collage of healthy, vibrant, youthful bodies, motivates me to take better care of myself and provides me with a visual model.

If you want to try this, be sure the pictures you choose are realistic for your body type and reflect your values. For example, don't choose a picture of someone with long legs if yours aren't long or of a body that is in a sexy pose unless that is the attitude you want to cultivate. Better yet, if you have a picture of yourself as you'd like to be, use that. Be sure to include appropriate affirmations. In this case, the affirmation might be: "I am healthy, vibrant, and youthful. I give thanks for my healthy, strong body."

I even have successfully manifested material things with treasure maps, and many do use them for this. When my husband and I moved into our first apartment and needed furniture, I cut out pictures of furniture and wrote across the collage: "I give thanks for my lovely new furniture!" (Giving thanks for things not yet manifest helps them manifest.) I put that treasure map in a prominent place, and each time I looked at it, I felt the excitement and pleasure of already having that furniture. Three days later, an old bank account that my husband's grandmother had been keeping for him since he was a child was discovered and turned over to him with just the right amount of money. This and other similar incidents have demonstrated to me the power of visualization and affirmation. We are creators!

Clearing is a technique for discovering the negative beliefs that may be preventing us from manifesting what we are visualizing and affirming. It is done by writing down an affirmation repeatedly and then attending to the doubts, fears, or negative thoughts aroused during this process. You attend to that little voice that says "but…", and you write down those "buts." But I don't deserve it, but there isn't enough money, but I'm too old, but I'm not good enough, etc. You can do this by dividing a piece of paper in half vertically and writing the affirmation on the left and your "buts" on the right. Or you can use a separate sheet for each.

When you are all finished, you will be able to see the blocks you create to your own happiness. You will also discover disparaging phrases that you have internalized from parents and others, which block your happiness. Just making these negative beliefs conscious may be enough to keep them from interfering; however, you may need to do some work around them, perhaps by creating affirmations to counteract them. Psychotherapy may even be necessary to work through some of them.

Relaxation

Any visualization work you do will be enhanced by first learning to relax. Your visualization work will only be as potent as your ability to relax and involve yourself fully in it. This alone is reason to learn relaxation, but relaxation has other benefits as well. It has a powerful potential for healing in other ways, with results similar to meditation. When we are deeply relaxed, oxygen consumption, lactate levels, and heart rate all decrease; respiration is slowed; and alpha waves are produced in the brain. We feel calm, peaceful, and refreshed.

These physiological changes combat stress and high blood pressure, and consequently their related diseases, heart attack and stroke. Dean Ornish, M.D., a cardiologist, also found that relaxation was a factor in lowering cholesterol levels. Joan Borysenko, Ph.D., a pioneer in the new science of psychoneuroimmunology (which studies the relationship between the mind, the nervous system, and the immune system), has shown that many diabetics can manage with less insulin when they practice relaxation. People with chronic pain and asthma also have experienced some relief through relaxation. [2]

Another way relaxation benefits the healing process is by stilling the mind, which allows messages from the Higher Self to be received intuitively. An added benefit is that the more often relaxation is practiced, the easier it is to feel relaxed even under stressful conditions. So, with sufficient practice in relaxation, it is possible to live a healthy and peaceful life even amidst stressful circumstances. As the stress in our lives increases, it becomes all the more imperative that we find ways that help us live with stress without it adversely affecting our health.

Fortunately, relaxation is a skill that can be learned. One way to learn it is through a method called progressive relaxation. Here is an example of a progressive relaxation exercise for teaching the art of relaxation:

Settle comfortably into your chair. Feel your body sink into its softness. Feel your body becoming heavier and heavier as it relaxes into the softness of the chair.

Now, focus your awareness on your head. Feel the heaviness of your head where it rests on the chair. Feel your head sinking even more deeply into the softness of the chair. Releasing all tension in your head, visualize any worries drifting away like so many bubbles... drifting away, so that all you are left with is peace and relaxation. Imagine this peace and relaxation spreading throughout your face... to your eyes... your nose... your cheeks... your mouth... your chin... your neck... releasing the tension like so many bubbles, releasing and relaxing into the glorious feeling of peace and relaxation that is yours anytime. Feel the results of relaxation through your entire head area.

Now, imagine this peace and relaxation spreading to your upper chest... your heart region... your stomach... your sides. Feel yourself immersed in feelings of relaxation and peace as all tension in these areas is released like bubbles, floating away softly, easily, effortlessly. Feel the deep sense of relaxation that results after all tension is released. Feel it spreading and penetrating every cell of your body in this area.

Now, imagine this peace and relaxation spreading to your upper arms... your elbows... your lower arms... and your hands. Feel each finger loosen and relax as tension is released. Feel the tension released throughout your arms and hands like tiny bubbles, effortlessly and easily. Feel the warmth, safety, comfort, and healing in the peaceful relaxation that is spreading now throughout your entire upper body.

Now, imagine this peace and relaxation spreading throughout your lower body, soothing and releasing any tension in this area, releasing any holding and gently enveloping this area in the warmth, safety, comfort, and peace of relaxation. Feel this relaxation spreading to your upper legs... your knees... your calves... your ankles... your feet... and your toes. Feel all tension in these areas released like tiny bubbles, effortlessly and easily, leaving behind only a peaceful sense of deep relaxation, comfort, and total safety. Rest a while in these feelings of total relaxation as they penetrate and deepen fully.

Some progressive relaxation exercises suggest tensing and then releasing each body part in succession. One is given on page 56 in *Healing Music* by Andrew Watson and Nevill Drury. *Healing Music,* although ostensibly about music, contains some excellent healing visualization exercises. It also gives suggestions for music to accompany your visualizations.

Trance Induction

Once some familiarity with relaxation is achieved, you are ready for visualization work, which is best preceded by a trance induction. A trance induction is used before visualization work to increase receptivity. It puts you into a light trance, which opens you up to receiving healing and insight. This light trance state is entered more easily the more accomplished you are at relaxation.

What follows is a trance induction to use before your visualizations. Many equally useful trance inductions are presented in other books. You will have to experiment to find one that suits you. This one represents a more transpersonal approach. It can be tape recorded and played back as a lead in to the visualization you plan to do. Be sure to record it in a slow, calm, evenly-paced voice. You may need to practice reading it a few times before you find a pace and tone of voice that works best for you.

Imagine that you are lying on a beach. The warm sand is beneath you . . . the sun is shining warmly on you . . . and a comfortable breeze brushes against you, gently caressing and soothing you. In the background, the rhythmic motion of the waves can be heard, lulling you into a wonderful dream-like state. Your only awareness is of the warm sand beneath you, the warmth of the sun, the gentle breeze brushing across your body, and the sound of the waves. Nothing else exists in your awareness but the warm sand beneath you... the sun... the breeze... and the waves. Rest in this place a moment and allow this reality to penetrate and engulf you.

As you lie there, you become aware of another sensation. It's not like any sensation you have ever had. It's like a yearning, but different. You feel this yearning sensation deep inside your being with your heart as its center. It's so compelling that it absorbs your entire awareness now. Only this sensation in the area of your heart exists, and its meaning is beginning to become clear.

You become aware of a deep, penetrating Light in the area of your heart center... a shaft of Light penetrating into your heart center. And you realize that the yearning is this shaft of Light that is burning deeply into your heart, warming it, opening it, piercing it with its indescribable love. The love from this shaft is filling the space around you... expanding... and moving outward to include the entire universe. As you remain engulfed in this Light—this love—feeling its strength and compassion, you realize that you are this Light. You are this love. It is not only entering your body but also pervading and permeating every cell of your body, healing it, cleansing it, and freeing it from all fear... all tension... all pain... healing it and enfolding it in its immense love, compassion, and peace. Rest a moment in this Light.

This induction has the advantage of opening you up to the Self and beginning the work of healing on deeper levels. The experience of the Light is not a fantasy but a reality. Imagining the Light entering your body, healing it, and pervading it with love is an invitation for it to do this. This simple induction sets in motion the profound healing process that is available for the asking.

The visualizations that follow should be preceded by progressive relaxation or a trance induction. They can be tape recorded and played back whenever you feel the need for them. They should be recorded in a slow, calm voice and listened to while reclining in a relaxed state. When making a tape for yourself, be sure to fit the images and gender to yourself. For instance, don't include daisies if you don't like them or bees if you have an insect phobia.

Visualizations for Eliminating Blocks

The following visualization can be used any time fear and negativity are blocking success or happiness.

As you lie there relaxing deeply, let an image come to mind of yourself as you would like to be. Take as long as you need to fill in the details of this image. What are you wearing? How are you standing? What is the look on your face? Above all, how are you feeling? (pause)

Now, allow this new image of yourself to tell the you that is lying here how it feels to be this new you. Continue to just feel how it feels to be this new you. (Allow a minute or two to pass.)

Now, bring to mind whatever is standing in the way of experiencing yourself like this all the time. (pause)

Now, experiment with it. First, make it very big. Now, make it very small. Now, make it even smaller. Now, give it a smiley face and crossed eyes. Dress it up in something outrageous. Color it blue and make it stand on its head. Now, tell it that you have had enough fun with it today and it can leave. Wave goodbye to it as it departs. Watch it become smaller and smaller as it leaves, waving to you all the way.

It may be hard to appreciate the power of visualizations if you have never used them. Although they may seem silly to the conscious mind, they affect the unconscious similar to past-life therapy. Like past-life regression, visualizations reprogram the unconscious, the seat of our fears. This particular visualization demonstrates that we have the power to affect what we fear. When we no longer feel powerless to affect our fear, it diminishes. Through a visualization of this type, we are empowered with the weapon of our own imagination. With the help of the imagination, a fear can be erased or diminished to a manageable size.

Another issue for many is the inability to achieve their goals. When we unconsciously sabotage our goals, a visualization that symbolizes moving smoothly past blocks may be helpful in freeing unconscious limitations placed on ourselves, once it is determined that our goals are appropriate:

Imagine that you are moving quietly and effortlessly across a vast expanse of land. You are gliding above the smooth land, propelled by your desire to move. You aren't sure why you feel compelled to go, but you are. Feel yourself skimming over the distance, smoothly and effortlessly, easily, like it was second nature to you, as if you had no will involved in it at all. Nothing is stopping you, and nothing is slowing you down or making work out of this journey. It is happening of its own accord and in its own time. Soon you will have arrived at your destination, and it will seem as if you had hardly begun your journey. Soon you will have what you came for, and the journey will end as easily and smoothly as it began. Rest a moment in these reflections, feeling the ease and satisfaction in this journey.

A blockage in the aura reflecting an unconscious attitude may actually be dissolved by a visualization like this one. When healing is accomplished on an unconscious level through visualization, it will be reflected in the aura. Working this way may seem a bit magical, but the unconscious is a mysterious aspect of ourselves. Sometimes symbolic means, like the example above, can get to the root of an issue more effectively than conscious means. As you can imagine, finding a suitable visualization is quite an art. You have to approach visualizations with an experimental attitude, trying various ones until you find one that works. Following up visualizations like these with appropriate affirmations enhances their effectiveness.

Visualization to Counteract Feelings of Worthlessness

Feeling worthless or inadequate is another common difficulty that also responds well to visualization work supported by affirmations. What follows is a visualization that can be used to counteract these debilitating feelings:

Relaxing now as deeply as you can, imagine that you are on a boat. Feel the shifting of the boat, back and forth, back and forth, as it lulls you gently into deep relaxation. As you move deeply into relaxation, you become aware of a Light in the distance. The Light draws you to it with its brilliance and beauty. There is something else about this Light . . . a sense of peace, tranquillity, and total and unconditional love. It is the love emanating from this Light that draws you closer and closer. As you approach the Light, you feel its warmth envelop you, cradling you in its comforting brilliance. It will not be long before it totally envelops you, and you will be able to rest in its love and peace indefinitely. See yourself moving slowly toward this Light. Feel it penetrating into every pore of your body.

Feel the Light's special significance for you at this time in your life. Know that this Light is meant especially for you, for your healing and refreshment. Know that you can immerse yourself in this Light whenever you want. Know that this Light will always be available to you no matter where you are, no matter how tired you are, no matter how forlorn you are. All you have to do is summon this Light to you and it will come. Rest in this Light for a while.

Visualization for Perspective

Life is painful, but the pain holds many lessons for us. However, it is hard to learn from pain when we are caught inside it. Before pain's lessons can be integrated, we need to be able to step back from it, understand it, embrace it, and not blame ourselves for it. Imagery work can help us gain some distance from our painful feelings.

Imagery work also may bring us an experience of our Higher Self, which helps us live more comfortably with life's imperfections. As we bask in the awareness of our Higher Self, our worries diminish. We still feel the pain, but it is more distant, less personal. As a result, although we may not be able to change a disturbing circumstance, we can live with it more gracefully. From this perspective, we understand that life is a play, with ourselves as the actor and the writer.

The following visualization can help us gain this perspective:

Imagine that you are floating above your body, looking down at this individual you know to be you lying in the chair. Experience what it would be like to observe you for the first time, having never set eyes on a human being before. Observe this individual uncritically and with the deepest sense of curiosity and wonder. Observe the placement of the features on the face, the expression. Don't try to know what this individual is feeling now . . . just observe, as if you were someone from another galaxy, curious about the life forms on this planet. What are these features? What do they do? How do they function? Allow your gaze to travel over every inch of this body in front of you, observing it, knowing it is alive, but without understanding it completely. Observe this individual another minute or so from this dispassionate stance.

As you gaze at this individual, your vision shifts and you become aware of another dimension. You are aware of a magnificent Light surrounding and interpenetrating the materialized body. It is glowing and alive with vibrancy, love, and life. You realize that the materialized portion of this individual is a crude manifestation of the Light surrounding it. It is focalized energy that is serving some function for this larger body of Light. How strange, you think. In relation to the Light, this materialized form seems insignificant. As insignificant as it seems in comparison to the greater Light-body, you also sense a deep and intense love being showered on it. It is nestled in the womb of this greater Light-body, being sheltered and cared for by it with intense and unwavering unconditional love. Rest a moment in this image, and feel the presence of your Higher Self.

Visualization for Embracing Challenge

Visualizations also can be used to counteract blame or resentment over an illness or difficulty. A visualization like the following one can be used to introduce the possibility of an illness or other problem having a purpose in our life:

Relax and breathe deeply. Close your eyes and allow yourself to relax deeply into the imagery. Soon you will feel yourself becoming absorbed in this world being created within you by these words. Allow these words to penetrate to the deepest parts of you to help you in your healing. You are about to embark on an inner journey to soothe and heal you. It will be as pleasurable as you allow it to be. Let's begin by going deeper inside, into a world where only images created by these words exist.

Once upon a time there was a girl (or boy) who felt happy and free and full of life. She loved to roll in the grass, splash in puddles, and swing from trees. She spent the warm summer days swimming in a quiet pond, far away from the noise of the busy world. In this special place, she could dive in the water and feel its coolness wash over her body, relaxing and refreshing her.

One day she discovered a beautiful green pasture not too far from her favorite swimming hole. There she saw butterflies lazily floating from one flower to another and tall grasses shifting lightly in the wind. When she stayed very still, she could hear the grasses moving in the wind, the bees humming, and the birds singing in the distance to each other. The pasture was alive with life. She could smell it too. She smelled the sweet grasses, the earth, even the flowers that dotted the pasture with their delicate colors: blue cornflowers, yellow and white daisies, lavender and magenta flowers too. She felt the sun like a warm cloak around her, gently soothing her with its delightful warmth. She decided to rest in this pasture, and found a soft grassy spot where she could be very comfortable. Soon she was relaxing deeply into this wonderfully quiet and peaceful place.

Then she began to dream. She dreamed of a far-off land where kings and queens ruled the land. The king and queen of this land were benevolent and generous. One day a girl (or boy) came to the king and queen and asked to take on a difficult mission that would benefit herself and the entire kingdom. The king and queen gave her permission, for they saw she had the strength and determination to succeed. They sent her off lovingly, knowing she would return and all would be better for it.

The girl knew this too. However, once off on her own and alone in the woods, she faced creatures she had never seen before, and she began to wonder if she could carry out this mission. At times she forgot why she took on this task, and her strength and determination waned. But even in her weakest moments, something inside her remembered and remained strong, confident, and resolute.

She learned to listen to this courageous part of herself instead of her frightened self. Whenever she was afraid, she called on this triumphant, strong, and confident part. Each step of her journey became easier as she regained the sense she had had of herself before she began and she recalled the importance of her mission. These remembrances fueled her courage, so even when things were difficult, she accepted this as part of her chosen destiny.

You too, (name), have taken on a difficult challenge. Sometimes you think you won't make it through it. You think that God is punishing you and that you don't deserve to be treated this way. And that's true. You don't deserve pain and difficulty, but you have chosen it to accomplish something. Like the girl (boy), you have chosen this challenge, because you will be better for it. But you have forgotten you made this choice.

A part of you remembers choosing this and rejoices in it. A part of you is up to this challenge and embraces it as the finest thing you can do. Embrace this challenge, know that you have chosen it, and ask for the help you need from the part of you that remembers this choice and wants to help you with it. You have everything you need to succeed, but you have to ask for help from this part that has perfect wisdom, love, and understanding. This higher aspect of yourself will guide you, so that you can benefit from this challenge.

Rest in this experience for a while (about five minutes).

Visualization for Weight Reduction

Creative visualization also can help us change our behavior. One common use of creative visualization is for weight control or reduction. Although the many conscious and unconscious factors contributing to weight gain need to be pinpointed before creating an individualized program of visualization and visualization may not be effective for everyone, for many the simple act of visualizing what they want to look and feel like is enough to create the motivation necessary to lose weight.

For instance, resting quietly for about fifteen minutes several times a day while imagining ourselves as we would like to be will reinforce our desire to lose weight. We should imagine ourselves becoming not only more slender but also more beautiful, confident, poised, and healthy. The importance of desire as a fuel for achieving our goals should not be underestimated. Many of us who are overweight have reinforced our desire for food. It makes sense, then, that reinforcing a different desire will help overcome an inordinate desire for food.

Visualizations also can be created to address specific issues contributing to a weight problem. For instance, some people use a weight problem as a buffer from the world. On an unconscious level, they may feel that if they are overweight they will not need to compete on other levels, having already proven their lack of worth to themselves and to others by being overweight. This is untrue, of course, and undermines their potential. However, believing this can be easier than facing the possibility of failure. When this is what is going on, imagining themselves as thinner and more beautiful may not be enough to lose weight because of the payoff in remaining overweight. Consequently, any unconscious belief or attitude that may sabotage progress must be identified and then addressed in a visualization designed to counteract it. The following is an example of a visualization that can be used to overcome the desire to escape life by being overweight:

Imagine that you are resting in the bottom of a boat, lying quietly and comfortably, relaxing to the gentle rocking of the boat as it floats lazily and slowly on the water. The sun is shining warmly on you like a blanket. You can feel it on your face... your neck... your shoulders... your chest... your arms... your hands... your stomach... your legs... and your feet. Rest here a moment feeling the warmth of the sun on your whole body and the gentle rocking of the boat.

Imagine that you are gazing at yourself as your guardian angel might, as your soul might, with total compassion and acceptance. Any feelings of judgment have completely dissolved as you gaze at yourself from this perspective. You don't need to do anything or change anything about yourself to make yourself more acceptable. You don't need to strive for anything or try to be anything. Being alive and feeling your aliveness is enough. Feel yourself at total peace and harmony with who you are. Feel the sense of love and acceptance your soul has for you at this very moment. Your soul experiences nothing but joy in beholding your aliveness and the perfection of your existence. Rest a moment now and allow yourself to feel the total acceptance and love that are being showered on you at this time.

Continue to see yourself from the perspective of your soul, or your guardian angel. Your soul rejoices in your choice to be born into a body at this time. It rejoices in this opportunity to be alive. It rejoices

in the opportunity it has through you to grow in greater understanding, wisdom, and love. Through you it has the opportunity to
experience life in physical form. Looking out through your eyes, it
sees the immense beauty and aliveness of three dimensional existence. It sees every form dancing with brilliance, aliveness, and joy in
its existence. Feel the aliveness that your soul is experiencing now,
the joy... the love... and the beauty it is experiencing now because of
your rebirth into a physical body. You are inherently beautiful...
perfect... whole. You are inherently all this... all the aliveness...all the
beauty... all the joy... and all the love. You are this.

You are all this, but you have chosen to express yourself in the
form you know as (name). You are not this form. It is just one of your
many forms—a temporary one—a form you have taken on to allow
you to play in this three dimensional realm, a form that allows you to
explore this realm. You will be this form for a while . . . but only for a
while. Someday you will return to your Wholeness beyond the physical realm where you know yourself as All That Is. Rest with these
thoughts a moment. Experience their truth in the deepest parts of
your being. And when you are ready to return to this plane of illu-
sion, you can open your eyes and be (name) again.

This visualization used repeatedly can bring us the experience of our Higher Self, an experience that is ever available if
we are open to it. This experience is a profound one with
profound ramifications for healing, it being the single most
important factor in promoting emotional healing and well-
being.

Any means for altering our consciousness has the same
potential for promoting healing as this visualization. Music is
another way to alter consciousness and can be a powerful tool
in the healing process. More will be said about music in the
next chapter. What is important is that the means used for
altering consciousness is enjoyable.

Another block to losing weight for some is the fear that they
will not be able to handle their new appearance gracefully. At
the root of this fear may be a negative belief about what being
thin will mean for them. They may be afraid of becoming sexu-
ally provocative, arrogant, unmotherly, or superficial. The
earlier visualization that suggested envisioning oneself as
becoming more confident, beautiful, healthy, and poised while
becoming thinner would need to be modified for them to
include kindness and other virtues feared to be lost if they
became thin. Our underlying attitudes and beliefs related to the

desired change need to be examined carefully and visualizations adjusted accordingly.

Visualization for Problem-Solving

The following shows how a traditional problem-solving technique can be coupled with a trance state to achieve results
more effectively:

Imagine that you are on a boat that is drifting slowly downstream.
You feel the sunshine on your face . . . your neck . . . your shoulders
. . . your chest . . . your arms . . . your hands . . . your stomach . . .
your legs . . . and your feet. As you completely relax into the gentle
rhythmic rocking of the boat, you begin to dream.

You dream that you are in a parade, and everyone in the parade is
dressed in a costume as something they'd like to be. There is
someone dressed like a ballerina . . . a doctor . . . a violinist . . . a
professor . . . a clown. Picture yourself as you'd dress in this parade.

Now, imagine what it would take for you to become this. Imagine
each stage of the process as if you were watching a slow-motion film
of the unfolding of this occupation. Where are you in this process?
What remains undone? What will it take? Are you willing to do that?
(If not, envision another costume and repeat the procedure.) What
might stand in the way of accomplishing your plan? How will you
deal with that? Examine all the blocks that might arise at the various
stages of your plan and see what your options are at each of these
points.

Visualizations for Experiencing Your Higher Self

Here are two visualizations that will help you experience the
Light and love of your Higher Self:

Feel the relaxation permeating and penetrating your entire body,
leaving you with only feelings of peace, acceptance, comfort, and
love. Notice how these feelings deepen as your relaxation deepens.
Notice how they can actually be felt in your body. You can feel the
energy of these feelings as bodily sensations. Worry and fear cannot
compete with the sense of peace, love, serenity, and absolute calm
and acceptance pervading you right now. These feelings are those of
your Higher Self. Your Higher Self is this total, unconditional love.
When you are feeling this way, you are actually experiencing yourself
as your Higher Self. Know that this is you in another state . . . a state

beyond the personality. You are this peace . . . this love . . . this acceptance. And anytime you want to experience this, all you have to do is take the time to lie still, relax, and invite it. This is your birthright, your true nature . . . You. Rest a moment in these feelings and get to know them. Get to know yourself beyond the personality you know as (name), for you are much more . . . so much more.

Imagine that you are a star, sparkling and shining with the light of the universe. Around you are other points of light scattered in the distance. They seem so distant, so distinct from yourself. In the vastness of the universe, you feel small, insignificant, alone. From the earth's vantage point, however, you aren't distant and apart from the other stars, but part of an elaborate pattern of stars, moving in preordained simplicity and perfect harmony.

Most of the time you, (name), are like this star in feeling separate, alone, insignificant, and unnoticed. From the vantage point of God, however, you are not separate or insignificant but part of a larger, immensely complex, and incomprehensibly perfect plan... . Without you, the plan would be altered totally. You are that important. Rest a moment in this realization of your perfect place within the plan, of your significance to All That Is, to God, to the universe.

Repeated work with relaxation and suggestions of this nature may be necessary to reinforce the process of opening up. The following is another visualization that may be helpful:

Imagine that you are a bird. As this bird, you are able to fly from place to place and observe the activities of people and other living things. One day, while observing a gathering of people, you see a woman (man) who isn't participating in the group. She's sitting apart from the group—alone. You feel compassion for her, being a creature who travels in flocks, and you decide to try to communicate this compassion to her. Not knowing how, but determined to show her you care, you sweep down and try to land on her shoulder. Instead, she jumps up in alarm and frightens you away. You realize you didn't get your message across, so you call out to her in song, but she doesn't hear you. Finally, you settle for just sending her your compassion, hoping that someday she might become aware of it.

There is a part of you that has total, unconditional love and compassion for you. It feels totally accepting and loving toward you. It is always there, showering this love and compassion on you. Even your not being aware of this flow of love doesn't stop it or slow it down, doesn't daunt this part of you whose only purpose, whose very nature, is to send you love every moment of your life.

By becoming aware of the love being sent you, you can enjoy it and partake in it. You can use it for your own healing or send it to others for theirs. All you have to do is acknowledge the presence of this love in your life and the power it has to heal you and affect you for the good. A simple statement like, "I am open to receiving divine love (or the love of God)" will allow it to come pouring into your life. Ask for this and feel its presence for a while. It is a tangible experience.

Guided Visualization

Guided visualization is a specific kind of visualization: an inner journey taken to retrieve information from our Higher Self. Both creative visualization and guided visualization use inner imagery for healing, but their specific roles in the healing process are different. Creative visualization helps us make changes through active inner participation in creating these changes, whereas guided visualization is a method for receiving information to design these changes. Guided visualization can help us determine an appropriate direction, so that we can put our creative energy to work in keeping with our plan. Thus, guided visualization can help lay the foundation for creative visualization.

In seeking information from the Higher Self in a guided visualization, a symbolic form of the Higher Self is met and addressed in the journey. The form might be an old wise woman or man, a glowing light, a religious figure like Jesus, or any other symbol you like.

The following is an example of a basic guided journey that can be tape recorded and played back whenever you are in need of guidance. Once you are deeply relaxed, perhaps by first listening to a trance induction, the journey can begin:

As you take the first step of this journey, you are aware of an excitement, an anticipation of what is to come. You sense that this journey is significant. It is not just any journey but a pilgrimage, a mission to uncover the answer to your question, a question you have held in your heart long enough. You feel a sense of urgency and importance in asking this question now. You know that it's time for the answer to be made known to you, but like the pilgrimages of old, you must first journey to the sacred place to receive it.

With each step of this journey your question will become clearer. You will be able to ponder it from all angles, to embrace it as your own. Whatever the answer, you will be ready to receive it, because you know it is from a high source, a source you can trust, a source that will not betray you or mislead you. It is good to know that a place like this exists, a place in which truth can be found: your truth.

So, let's begin the journey. With the question in mind, you begin your journey, full of hope and promise for greater peace and understanding at its end. You begin your journey at the bottom of a steep mountain covered with the bright green grasses of springtime and sprinkled with flowers of radiant hues. Warm breezes are brushing against your face, the sun is shining promisingly, and birds are singing happily—joyously—oblivious of the importance of this day to you. To them, it's like any other day, but a particularly glorious one at that.

You begin your trek up the mountain, wondering as you go how long it will take. You decide to just keep your attention on your steps, on the green below your feet, on the song of the birds, on the smell and feel of the breeze, and on the sunshine on your face. Each step takes you closer to your destination. With each step you feel lighter, more alive, more joyous than ever before. Something magical is in the air that gives you the feeling you are walking along a special path, one trodden by many, but one that is yours alone today. You feel the dirt give way softly under your feet and you smell its earthy smell, as after a new rain. The grasses, the flowers, the breeze all have a characteristic smell: sweet, earthy, and alive.

You gaze behind you, and you see that you are nearly halfway up the mountain, nearly halfway to your destination. It's getting easier and easier, as you are feeling lighter and more joyous than ever before. Soon you will be there; soon you will arrive. But for now, you have the soft dirt beneath your feet, the sunshine on your face, the smell of the earth, and the breezes blowing softly, cooling you and bringing the sweetness of the mountain to you.

As you continue your climb, you realize that the air is changing. It's becoming softer, more ethereal. The air feels magical. Even the coloring is changing. You are beginning to be aware of soft purples, blues, and an iridescence about the light, as if it was shot through with rainbows, with fairy dust, with moonbeams. You sense that you will soon be approaching the sacred spot, and you stop a moment to compose yourself.

As you stop and rest, you turn inward with your question. Take a moment to word your question carefully so that it is clearly stated. (pause)

Now you begin again. You can see your destination, but for now it just looks like the top of the mountain, the end of the path. You can't tell what is ahead. You don't know what this sacred place looks like yet, but soon you will find out. You are taking your final steps now, approaching the top, and soon you will arrive. When you have arrived, take time to look around and absorb what you see. Take it in with all your senses, taking plenty of time to do this.

Now, find a place to be seated in this sacred space, one where you will be most comfortable, one that feels just right to you. (pause)

Now you are ready to meet (the old wise woman, the Virgin Mary, Jesus, your spirit guide, your Higher Self, etc.) who resides in this sacred place and will answer your question. You wait quietly for the arrival of this great Being. (pause)

It is nearly time to ask your question. You can speak to this Being as you would to any friend or mentor. Take as long as you need to receive and clarify the answer. Feel free to discuss any aspect of the answer that may be unclear. Ask your question now. (pause)

You return down the mountain the same way you came, but refreshed and with renewed vitality. Know that with each step, you are returning with more joy, more love, and more wisdom than you had when you began. Know that you can return to this place whenever you want. This sacred place is eternal and always available to you. There are no rules about how often you can visit it or how to approach it. All you need is a sincere question. Continue to take your time down the mountain, step by step, and when you have returned to the bottom of the mountain, to the green grasses at the foot of the mountain, you can open your eyes.

For most, it takes practice before this technique begins to work as effectively as it can. Don't be afraid to take this journey again if you feel dissatisfied with what you received.

As in shamanic journeying, defining the journey's purpose and determining the question in advance are key to its success. When the issue and question are given thorough consideration, the chance of a helpful response increases. This may be because taking the time to do this confirms and reinforces the desire to understand. A sincere desire is important, just as it is in using divinatory tools such as the *I Ching*, the Runes, or the Tarot. The questions you raise in these journeys should be serious and compelling; journeying should not be used frivolously.

On the facing page are some questions you might ask in a guided journey (or of the I Ching, the Runes, or the Tarot):

Some questions are inappropriate: What should I do? Where should I move? What job will I get? Where should I look for an apartment? When should I sell my car? Who will buy my house?

Questions for a Guided Journey

♦ What is the best attitude or approach to take toward (my work, my relationship, my health, my financial situation, my parents, my early upbringing, the abuse, this loss, this situation)?

♦ What do I need to understand now about (my work, etc.)?

♦ What is the truth about (a choice) as a direction for me?

♦ What is the truth about (an issue)?

and any others that interfere with our making our own choices. Questions that can be answered by a "yes" or "no" are usually not appropriate either. They are too simplistic and make it too easy to let something outside ourselves make our decisions for us. The purpose for journeying or using a divinatory tool is to gain understanding so that we can make wiser choices. Those who are looking for someone or something to make a decision for them are better off staying away from these tools. Unfortunately, not everyone is aware of his or her motives.

Everyone has issues that can be helped with visualization work. We all have unconscious attitudes, beliefs, and fears that undermine our potential and prevent us from experiencing greater peace and happiness. Creative visualization and guided visualization are ways to include our Higher Self in our healing and transform the parts of ourselves that are blocking our creativity and joy. They also are a means of receiving insight about our plan, who we are, and where we are going. Both are valuable tools in our own self-healing and useful adjuncts to more formalized healing.

CHAPTER 4 NOTES

1. Michael Talbot, *The Holographic Universe* (New York: Harper Collins, 1991), p. 82-83.

2. Bernie S. Siegel, M.D., *"How to Heal Yourself! The Curing Power of Hope, Joy and Inner Peace,"* Redbook, June 1989, p. 156.

CHAPTER 4 SOURCES

Benson, Herbert. *The Relaxation Response.* Boston: G.K. Hall, 1976.

Gawain, Shakti. *Creative Visualization.* New York: Bantam Books, 1985.

Siegel, Bernie S., M.D. *Peace, Love and Healing: Bodymind Communication and the Path to Self-Healing: An Exploration.* New York: Harper & Row, 1989.

Talbot, Michael. *The Holographic Universe.* New York: Harper Collins, 1991.

CHAPTER 4 SUGGESTED READING

Bonny, Helen and Louis Savary. *Music and Your Mind.* New York: Harper & Row, 1973.

Hay, Louise L. *You Can Heal Your Life.* Carson, Calif.: Hay House, 1987.

Houston, Jean. *The Possible Human.* Los Angeles: Jeremy P. Tarcher, 1982.

Mariechild, Diane. *Mother Wit: A Guide to Healing and Psychic Development.* Freedom, Calif.: The Crossing Press, 1988.

Masters, Robert and Jean Houston. *Mind Games.* New York: Dell, 1972.

Proto, Louis. *Self-Healing: Use Your Mind to Heal Your Body.* York Beach, Maine: Samuel Weiser, 1991.

Rossman, Martin L., M.D. *Healing Yourself: A Step-By-Step Program for Better Health Through Imagery.* New York: Simon & Schuster, 1987.

Scolastico, Ron, Ph.D. *Healing the Heart, Healing the Body: A Spiritual Perspective on Emotional, Mental, and Physical Health.* Carson, Calif.: Hay House, 1992.

Watson, Andrew and Nevill Drury. *Healing Music: The Harmonic Path to Inner Wholeness.* Garden City Park, N.Y.: Avery Publishing Group, 1987.

RESOURCES FOR AFFIRMATIONS

Hay House, Inc.
P.O. Box 6204
Carson, CA 90749-6204

Unity School of Christianity
Unity Village, MO 64065-0001

CHAPTER 5
Healing with Music, Movement and Art

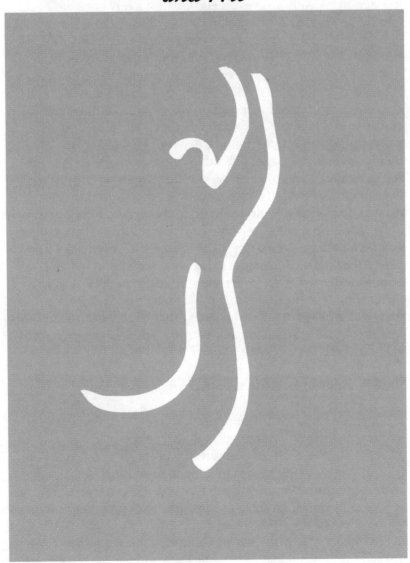

Self-expression is healing. The creative arts are healing, because they are, each in their own way, a means of expressing ourselves. The arts give people a way to say "This is who I am, this is how I feel, and this is what I believe." They are a vehicle for emotional expression and personal will, but more importantly, also for higher Will. They are a vehicle for expressing our truth and accessing Spirit.

The Self asserts itself through our individuality as surely as the ego does. Although even ego-expression is important and can be healing, Self-expression heals not only the artist but the collective. The Self uses artists to accomplish collective deeds. When the Self's will is expressed in music, art, and movement, it inspires people to act in a way that benefits the collective. When the creative artist successfully expresses the Self for the collective, the masses respond on deep levels and the artist is considered a genius. Less famous artists may be serving a similar purpose, but the masses may not be awakened yet to their particular message. Still other artists are only expressing the personal self in their work, but that serves a purpose too—in their own growth. Even they may be recognized by the masses if enough people resonate to that level of expression.

Much of the healing power of creativity comes from making what is unconscious conscious and from the expression—or externalization—of feelings. Expressing feelings is healing, as long as it doesn't hurt others. But the real power of creativity for healing is in its ability to align us with our Self. By expressing ourselves, we almost invariably express our Self too, at least partially. So, through creativity, Self is discovered and given a voice.

Well-Springs: a holistic creative arts experience

Recently, I was fortunate enough to meet Kay Ortmans, an internationally-known innovator in the field of creative arts therapy and the founder and director of the Well-Springs Foundation. Well-Springs' purpose is to foster healing, self-awareness, and spiritual growth through the creative arts. It serves individuals, groups, and families; and provides training for professionals.

Kay received her training in London at the Royal Academy of Music and the Dalcroze School of Eurhythmics, and in Germany

Three Ways Creative Expression Heals Us

1. By giving expression to feelings and thus undoing or avoiding repression, which causes depression and loss of contact with the Self,

2. By giving expression to the Self and thus discovering our higher nature. Creativity can be a way of affirming our higher nature and opening up to it.

3. Through the creativity of others. Artists uplift and inspire those of us who are not actively creating. We gain vicariously from those who express the Self through their art, music, or movement.

at the Rudolf Steiner School of Gymnastics. In the early 1960's, after many years of teaching, she developed the techniques she uses at Well-Springs. She combines art, music, movement, journaling, meditation, and massage to transform negative feelings, release creative potential, and access Spirit.

Well-Springs' goal is "to free the spirit through the body."[1] It is founded on the idea that the body knows what needs healing, and movement to music initiates and supports a process of healthy release. Since negative emotions and traumas often become stored in the body (even from past lives), creating tension, it makes sense that movement and stretching will help liberate them. As they are released, so is insight about their origin and energy that can be put to more productive use. This, of course, also is the premise of the body therapies, which seek to unlock stored pain and trauma through massage and other forms of physical manipulation. Music facilitates this process, because the altered state of consciousness it induces makes it easier for unconscious material to surface and be accepted.

Here is how Kay describes the process she uses with groups:

First we increase our own energy level through moving the body to fine music—letting go and allowing the wisdom of the body to take over and enjoy liberating ourselves with music and color. Merely walking around the room with vital energy starts the process of spiritual unfoldment. Then we add colored fabrics to the movement for the deep association colors have with past experiences and deep patterns. Dancing the body will help old vibrations escape and bring in a deeper peace, and new growth can emerge... .

When the energy level is high enough to allow situations to come up from the unconscious naturally, we turn to chalk drawing and working with clay to express out our feelings even further. Subtle forms of release can take place in the art work, and we have a notebook handy to write down our new feelings to help make them permanent patterns in our lives.

We also use silence filled with fine music. By breathing with the phrases we let the energy build up and joy surface, ready to catch insight when it is unleashed, keeping it easy and light. [2]

Music, movement, journaling, meditation, and art are combined to create an uplifting experience, which takes place over about two hours. The experience begins with people coming to the group with the problems and negative feelings they wish to work on. Without discussing them, the group begins moving to music. The music is always classical, which Kay believes is best because of its high vibration, much of it having been spiritually inspired. The music is carefully selected and changed several times throughout the two hours.

After moving to music for a while, large colored pieces of fabric are introduced, which allow for greater expressiveness, imagination, and abandon. Following this, people record their experience in their journals, being careful not to get into their intellects as they do so. They are encouraged to just let their intuitions, feelings, and insights about the experience flow and to write down whatever comes to mind.

Then, they get up and move some more to music, in preparation for expressing themselves further in chalk or with clay. When they feel ready, they make as many pictures or sculptures as they need to. When working with chalk, they choose their colors intuitively and try to stay attuned to the music, allowing their creative expression to come from within—not from the intellect. The process is similar with the clay. The changes in attitude are often dramatically apparent in the series of pictures or sculptures, as negative feelings are transformed into joy.

When people are finished creating their pictures or sculptures, they record their experience in their journals, still to music. Then, there is a period of sharing of experiences, art work, and journal entries. People in the group share their impressions of each other's art work as well.

By the time this process is finished, negative feelings have cleared and insights often have emerged. Those who have not received any insights often receive them later. Regardless of whether or not insights emerge, the process of cleansing ourselves of negative feelings and aligning with Spirit is in itself healing, and intellectual understanding is not a prerequisite for this. This is not to diminish the value of insight, but insight is not always necessary for healing to occur and, in fact, it can get in the way.

The Well-Springs approach is something we all can do, as individuals or as families, whenever we feel stressed out, in conflict, confused, or taken over by a negative emotion. Simply putting dynamic classical or other quality music on and expressing our feelings through that music, then journaling, then expressing our feelings through art, and then journaling again can transform those negative energies into joy and bring us in touch with new insights about the problem. These tools help us get into a higher relationship with our feelings, leaving us feeling lighter and able to see the humor in our situation. We can use these tools to transform any negative emotion that arises instead of expressing these feelings in the ordinary, often destructive, ways.

And just how do we move to music? Your movements should bubble up from within without conscious thought or judgment. Set aside your mind to allow your body to speak and your intuition to flow. Try throwing up your arms and imagining yourself releasing negativity and drawing down whatever positive energy you need. Stretching and making sweeping movements with your arms and hands will help clear your energy field of negativity. Let yourself move freely and uninhibitedly.

Kay explains:

> We don't follow music as much as we allow it to take us where it wants to go… The energy of the music has a life of its own and it moves us from the inside and brings us the exact experience that we need to unfold the next step of our journey…we listen with our whole being and let the music into us. [3]

Kay also suggests noticing what kind of movements we tend to make: Are they tight and constricted, small or large, jerky or graceful, polite and unobtrusive? Paying attention to this can give us a clue about our psychodynamics. Also, Where are we tense? Where is there pain? What might that pain say? What might the movements we are making be saying to us? Asking these questions will help us relate our movements to our feelings. Furthermore, we need to keep asking ourselves these questions throughout the movement so that we don't miss any insights or just "wallow in" the experience, which can be as much of a pitfall as wallowing in intellectual analysis or emotions. [4]

MOVEMENT ACTIVITIES

Move any furniture if necessary to give yourself enough space. To avoid feeling self-conscious, these activities should be done alone or only with others who are joining in. Whooping, screaming, yelling, and singing are all acceptable accompaniments, as a means of releasing feelings. Let yourself go! Let yourself find the movement you need to make; your body knows how it needs to move if you let it. And don't forget to breathe freely and deeply.

You will find that after moving to music, it will be easier to write about your feelings. Writing them down immediately is important not only to capture them but to capture the insights that will be arising. So, be sure to allow some time for recording your experiences.

Use dynamic classical or other high vibrational music at full volume and have fun! Classical music selections are specified in *Let Go to Music, Rebound to Life,* which can be obtained from the address listed under Movement Resources at the end of this chapter.

Activity 1: Walking to Music

Get that Walkman out and just walk (or run), keeping pace with the beat! Choose music intuitively to fit your mood. If you want to be energized, choose energetic music; if you want to relax, choose peaceful music; if you want to feel devotion, choose devotional music. Be sure it is of a high vibration, that is, capable of evoking the higher emotions: joy, love, peace, devotion. Just walking to music can be healing—preferably in nature (need I mention that nature is healing?).

Activity 2: Adding Color

Adding large solid-colored pieces of fabric to your movement to music can enhance the experience, draw out additional insight, and spark the imagination. Use fabric that is large enough to wrap around yourself. Have available a variety of textures, weights, and colors (black, white, and dark colors too). Some smaller pieces of filmy fabric to use like streamers feels good sometimes too. Natural fibers work best, because they won't create so much static electricity.

Choose a piece of fabric whose color you are either intuitively drawn to or repelled by. Colors have symbolic meaning to us and can often draw out or represent our inner state or unconscious feelings. Use your piece of fabric as if it was an extension of yourself. If you feel like it, change colors during the experience, while continuing to move. You will find that your mood and feelings evolve as you express them. Slow music often brings out deeper awareness and richness. 5

Activity 3: Stretching

Using appropriate music, stretch your body in slow motion. Stretching the area of your body that is most tense, stiff, or uncomfortable will help you release tension and trapped negativity. If necessary, massage or hold and warm that area to loosen it up so that you can stretch even further. Keep activating this area through movement. As you do this, you may gain insight into the cause of the tension or block. Then write down your experience in your journal or carry out a written dialogue with the part of you that is or was tense. 6

Movement and Healing

For many of these benefits, how you move is not particularly important. For others, like improving physical health, what you do and how you do it will be important. In all cases, intention is primary. Your intention is your prayer, your invocation. If you intend health as you move, whatever movement you make will bring you greater health than without this intention. Intention, invocation, and affirmation make movement a powerful tool for healing.

Music

Because we are energy-beings, we are affected by sound, which also is energy—or vibration. Our atoms, cells, glands, and organs all vibrate to a certain frequency and therefore both react to and emit sound. As Pir Hazrat Inayat Khan, founder of the Sufi Order of the West, explains:

The whole mechanism, the muscles, the blood circulation, the nerves are all moved by the power of vibration. As there is resonance for every sound, so the human body is a living resonator for sound... Sound has an effect on each atom of the body, for each atom resounds. On all glands, on the circulation of the blood, and on pulsation, sound has an effect. [7]

That we are affected by sound and music hardly requires proof: Some music makes us sleepy, some makes us cry, some makes us dance. We delight in some sounds, such as the sound of birds, and cringe at others, such as the sound of chalk on a chalkboard. We are even affected by sound when we are not aware of it, since we resonate to it whether or not we are paying attention to it.

We also are aware of how music and sound can affect our moods—both positively and negatively. Some studies have shown that music's negative effects may run deeper than just this, however. For example, it has been found that those living near an airport are ill 20% more often than those not living near one. [8] In addition, Dr. John Diamond's research has led him to believe that certain rhythms, often present in rock music, can make us feel drained or weaker. [9] Dr. Alfred Tomatis, a French

Movement is Healing

♦ It provides a means for expressing and processing feelings so that they do not accumulate in the body or the aura and poison our health and well-being.

♦ It clears existing emotional blocks in the body and in the aura. Movement can be used to release feelings from the unconscious safely and without feeding them. It is not even necessary to understand what is being released. A lightness ensues, bringing greater freedom.

♦ Through its ability to alter consciousness, it provides a means for expressing and contacting the Self.

♦ It evokes joy, which we have seen is healing.

♦ It gets us out of our heads and takes us away from our everyday concerns.

♦ It relieves stress.

♦ It can affirm health and beauty. Making an effort to improve your health and beauty through movement of any kind affirms your desire for that, which evokes healing from Spirit.

♦ It oxygenates and conditions the body, improving physical health, agility, strength, and the circulation. This, in turn, manifests as greater confidence and well-being.

♦ It feels great! It leaves you feeling alert, energized, peaceful, and centered.

physician and psychologist, also found that certain sounds energize us, while others drain us. He studied Benedictine monks and discovered that daily chanting was necessary for them to maintain their rigorous schedules. When they stopped chanting, they became tired, depressed, and more subject to illness. [10]

We are also learning about music's positive effects. Of particular significance to healing is music's ability to evoke the relaxation response and all its benefits.

The power of music to heal lies not only in its power to relax us. The act of singing an uplifting song—one about universal love, for instance—actually evokes that love within us. Music is healing, because it evokes within us positive feelings such as joy, devotion, love, and peace. And as Dr. Bernie Siegel has shown, these positive emotions correlate with physical health.

Music is also a way of affirming our ideals and all we hold dear. Affirmations put to music align us with the truth, beauty, love, peace, or other ideals we are singing about and help these manifest in our life and in the world. Song used this way is a prayer—and a powerful one at that. We have seen how important asking for healing is to well-being because of its power to invoke the Light. Music has this same potential for

Music ...

♥ ...reduces stress.

♥ ...transports us to a more beautiful place, where we can transcend our troubles temporarily.

♥ ...quiets the mind.

♥ ...enhances imagery work.

♥ ...releases material from the unconscious and makes us more receptive to unconscious material.

♥ ...stimulates the intuitive, right-hemisphere of the brain and enhances creativity, intuition, and imagination.

♥ ...eases depression and anxiety, and diminishes pain.

♥ ...slows heart beat and breath; and improves functioning of the autonomic, immune, endocrine, and neuropeptide systems. [11]

invoking the Light.

Composing a song or a piece of music has even more power to heal than singing or playing someone else's compositions. Taking the time to do this proclaims our desire for healing and contact with the Self, just as composing our own affirmations does. Our own compositions also are more likely to express our feelings accurately than someone else's.

The real power of music for healing lies in its potential to shift our consciousness—to open us up to new dimensions of our being—and thus activate our own healing potential: Music acts as a bridge to our higher nature. The shift in consciousness, which happens because of harmonious vibrations that balance the aura, results in a surrender of ego-consciousness to soul-consciousness. Through this shift, we claim our sonship/daughtership to the Divine and gain access to our inherent healing power.

Music has been used to expand consciousness and access healing throughout history by nearly every culture. The discovery that music is healing is not a discovery at all—but a re-discovery on the part of Western civilization of what shamans and tribal peoples throughout the world have known for millennia. Their healing rituals have included the ingredients we are now discovering are healing. They use rhythm, drumming, dance, and song to alter consciousness in both the shaman and the patient, and increase the patient's receptivity to healing. They use music to uplift and inspire the patient too—to evoke feelings of hope and devotion. The ritual itself is designed to inspire the patients' faith in the shaman's ability to heal.

Balancing the Aura

Everything in the universe has a vibration, a tone underlying its beingness. Planets, stones, plants, animals, the wind, water, fire, earth, each contains an indigenous tonal expression characteristic of its energetic framework. [12]

We each have a note, or vibration, that is distinctive to us. Sounds that are inharmonious to this vibration can unbalance and harm us, whereas sounds that resonate with us restore our health. According to shamanic tradition, we also each have a "life song," which is our own secret song of personal power, as well as a "healing song," which enables us to heal ourselves and others. When we bring our being into resonance with our tone or song, health results. 13

Thus, an even more esoteric relationship exists between sound and healing. This relationship exists because both sound and healing operate through the medium of energy. The physical body is materialized energy with a less dense vibration of energy called the aura surrounding and interpenetrating it. Sound, of course, also is energy. When a blockage or irregularity in the aura reflects some form of dis-ease, feeding the aura with a certain frequency of vibration (sound) can erase the irregularity and return the aura to its natural state and the person to health. This clearing of the aura, or balancing as it is sometimes called, also results in a shift in consciousness, an altered state similar to that in meditation.

Health will remain if what caused the irregularity ceases. If not, the irregularity will return. Consequently, the cause of a problem must be eliminated to maintain the effects of healing with sound. Nevertheless, sound can be an effective adjunct to other methods that create deep, long-lasting changes.

In *The Book of Sound Therapy*, Olivea Dewhurst-Maddock provides a chart detailing the relationship between the notes of the scale and certain body parts, senses, and systems. She suggests that the functioning of that system or area of the body can be improved by singing chants in the note that corresponds to that system or part, and by exposing ourselves to sounds and music based on that note, including tuning forks, musical instruments, and toning. She and many others also have assigned the seven notes of the scale to the seven chakras, with C corresponding to the root chakra, D to the reproductive chakra, and so on, ending with B at the crown chakra.

Sound Meditation

Focusing on a piece of music can be an excellent introduction to meditation and expanded states of consciousness. Those whose primary mode is auditory and who enjoy music will be the ones most responsive to meditating on sound. Deep states of relaxation and shifts in consciousness can happen just by focusing on the sounds in a piece of music until those sounds are experienced bodily. Becoming completely absorbed in the sounds and the ensuing sense of relaxation is the goal of these meditations. A bodily experience of the sound indicates a deep level of involvement and can be used to deepen the meditation further by continuing to concentrate on the sound's bodily effect.

The amount of time needed to achieve this depth varies according to one's ability to remain focused, which increases with practice. A half hour is usually enough for most to benefit from sound meditation and certainly enough to create relaxation. Even if relaxation is all that is accomplished at first, sound meditation is worthwhile. Meditating on sound daily will enhance anyone's health and well-being.

Choosing Music for Meditation

If you are not experiencing deep relaxation or shifts in consciousness while meditating to music, it may not be due to a lack of focus but to the wrong choice of music. Unfortunately, there are no clear-cut answers to what music works best with whom: No one kind of music works for everyone or in every situation. What is relaxing or inspiring to one person may be annoying to another. So, you will have to use your intuition in selecting music and do some experimenting.

The new genre of music called *New Age music, meditation music, space music, or ambient music* has been created for healing, relaxing, and meditation. Much of the music in this genre has no recognizable melody or rhythm. Its sounds are directionless, undulating, and seemingly endless. Whereas most music seeks to elicit emotion through patterns that build and release (which, as we have seen, is useful for expressing and processing feelings), this music avoids eliciting emotion or stimulation of any kind. Instead, it seeks to soothe, quiet, and alter one's state of consciousness and mood. Steven Halpern is one of the main pioneers in this area, has written extensively about it, and has made numerous recordings.

On the following page are some general guidelines for selecting music for meditation. They reflect the principles behind New Age music.

Choosing Music for Meditation

♫ Choose music without words. Although music containing words can achieve the desired effect with regular meditators, words are likely to be distracting for beginners, since words tend to stimulate left-brain activity. The exception to this would be music, such as a Gregorian chant, which is based on a repetitive word or phrase.

♫ Choose music without extremes in tempo, volume, instrumentation, or melody, at least if you are a beginning meditator. This kind of music may seem bland to those used to more stimulating music. However, its purpose is to soothe and shift consciousness—not excite the emotions or entertain.

♫ Avoid music that evokes emotion, except higher emotions like unconditional love. Evocative music is often in a minor key, and contains extremes in range and frequent variations in tempo and volume. Some instruments are more evocative than others as well, particularly those with a high register, such as the violin and the flute. Music containing instruments with extremely high or low registers probably should be avoided.

♫ Choose music you like. This may contradict previous guidelines if you like rock music, for instance. Nevertheless, try to find music within these guidelines that appeals to you.

♫ Do choose music that evokes devotion, love, joy, and peace. Kiirtans (Indian devotional music), New Age music, shamanic drumming, and Gregorian chants or other sacred music are all suitable choices, assuming they appeal to you. You can even find tapes with only a mantra (a sacred phrase) on it.

♫ Choose music that makes you feel good. Let your feelings be your guide to the music that is best for you.

Chanting

It seems appropriate to give special mention to chanting, since it is a very ancient and healing type of vocalization. Chanting is a type of sound meditation in which a sound is meditated on as it is repeated in song. This sound is usually a sacred word or phrase, or a divine name, although it could be a whole hymn or prayer. Chanting, like meditation, focuses us in the present, which quiets our mind and alters our consciousness. It also invokes the Divine, and aligns us with and asserts our receptivity to the Divine. It has the additional benefit of producing sounds that in themselves have a healing effect on our aura and that of those with whom we are chanting, since chanting is often done with others. When it is done in a group, the power for healing is multiplied, as the energy of the members resonates as one.

Chanting has other benefits as well: It clears the fifth chakra (as does singing), relieves anxiety, dissipates fear and negativity, synchronizes brain waves, energizes, and brings mental clarity and tranquility.

There are even specific chants for clearing the chakras. A sacred sound, discovered by mystics during their meditations, corresponds to each chakra. Chanting this sound several times in a prescribed way clears that chakra. Other chants have also been found to clear the chakras. Laeh Maggie Garfield presents the specifics of how to use chanting to clear the chakras in her book *Sound Medicine: Healing with Music, Voice, and Song*.

Toning

Toning, also called overtone chanting, is an esoteric tradition that is centuries old. Toning uses vowel sounds to alter a person's vibration and restore him or her to harmony or wholeness. It is used to release emotional blocks in the aura, which results in mental clarity, tranquility, feelings of love, and a sense of well-being. Although toning offers therapeutic potential, it requires a teacher and an excellent intuition, since the process of finding the right note to tone for a particular individual or for oneself is an intuitive one. [14]

Music and Emotional Expression

As mentioned earlier in describing Well-Springs, music is a wonderful tool for helping us express and process feelings. Listening to a sad song or playing one on the piano, for instance, can be a healthy way of acknowledging, accepting, and expressing any sad feelings we have. Music has been used throughout time to release feelings of sadness and even anger as well as to express feelings of joy, love, and devotion.

One word of caution, though, about using music for emotional expression: When we express a feeling in song or through a musical instrument, or experience it by listening to music, we are affirming that feeling. Thus, singing about love can create more love in the world and singing about injustice can inspire us to uphold justice. However, a song that evokes self-pity may only reinforce self-pity and one that evokes sorrow may only strengthen that too unless handled properly. If we aren't careful, we may end up reinforcing rather than releasing our negative feelings through music.

Therefore, we must be careful about how we use music and what music we choose to help us express our feelings. (Country Western music might not be a good choice for getting over that broken heart.) There is a fine line between healthy acceptance and expression of a feeling and feeding it. Music should be used to process and release negative feelings, but not to feed them or evoke them unnecessarily. The test of whether a piece of music is serving your healing or not is in how you feel afterward: Do you feel better or worse? Using music successfully to express feelings requires a willingness to get into a higher relationship to those feelings once they are acknowledged, expressed, and accepted. This is where humor, playfulness, movement, and the right kind of music can help.

I'd like to close this section with a quote from Miriam Therese Winter, a Medical Mission Sister, author, and musician:

Wholeness, healing, integration: that is what the inner journey is about, and it happens when our inner and outer selves, when the world within us and the world around us, when the Creator, creation, and our own creativity merge and emerge as one. We experience this fleetingly through music. I feel it deeply, often through song. It is the closest I have ever come to wholeness, and I suspect to holiness as well. It is where I turn in search of healing, not to be alone in my isolation but in order to center myself within the Center of all my longing, within that Presence, that Power, where all that lives resides.[15]

Art and Healing

Art is a way of making what is unconscious conscious, which, as we have seen, is key to healing. Visual symbols are, in fact, the language of the unconscious, as evidenced in dreams and imagery work. By drawing, we externalize what is in our unconscious and make it concrete and visible, which alone is healing. Drawing provides a way for us to see our feelings, attitudes, beliefs, and thoughts so that we can examine what we are holding in our minds and what feelings lie buried.

This is important, because our negative thoughts, attitudes, and beliefs (and consequently our negative feelings) are often at the bottom of our problems and our unhappiness. What we manifest in our lives directly relates to these negative thoughts and feelings. Therefore, if we want to manifest something different, we must examine our thoughts and make a conscious effort to adjust them.

Drawing helps us clarify these thoughts and feelings, and specify what we want and don't want; it helps us define the problem and our feelings about it. Drawing a picture of how we feel about an aspect of our life (our job, our body, our health, a relationship, our finances, etc.) is a way of contacting our feelings about it and bringing out our hidden beliefs or attitudes related to it. Lucia Capacchione, in her wonderful book *The Picture of Health*, suggests taking this a step further and dialoguing (either in writing or out loud) with this picture to draw out its symbolic message.

After we have defined our feelings and the problem through drawing, we can then draw a picture of what we would like that area of our life to be like. By drawing what we want, we are making our dreams and wishes visible—we are concretizing them—and we are affirming our desire for what we want to manifest. This picture can then be used to motivate us to make the needed changes to achieve this. The picture is a concrete reminder of what we want to create. When used this way, drawing is a visual affirmation. And, like a verbal affirmation, a visual affirmation can help us stay focused on our goal.

Combining such a visual affirmation with verbal and written affirmations strengthens it even further. We can write affirmations across or alongside the picture and read them out loud whenever we look at the picture. This picture and the affirmations can be placed in a prominent place in our home to ensure that we give it plenty of attention. Re-creating our mental imagery through visual, verbal, and written affirmations this way is the first step in re-creating ourselves and our lives. We are creators! And we can use the creative process for just that—re-creating ourselves.

In *The Picture of Health*, Capacchione, an art therapist, provides activities like this and others that make use of drawing to express feelings, make the unconscious conscious, and contact the Self. I highly recommend this and other books of hers if you are interested in using art to heal or reshape your life. Also in it are activities that show you how to uncover what may be behind any physical symptoms or pain you may be experiencing. For instance, just drawing the symptom (a headache, a cold, a backache, hives, etc.) and dialoguing with it can be very revealing.

Drawing also allows us to express feelings and experiences that are difficult to express any other way but which may be necessary to express for our well-being. This is one reason art therapy has been so effective with children who have been abused or traumatized, for whom verbal and more intellectual means of expression are more difficult. For the same reason, art therapy has been effective with the developmentally disabled and mentally ill. Just expressing our feelings is healing, even if we do no more than this. Here is an activity for expressing your feelings:

Gather your art materials (crayons, markers, and chalk or anything free-flowing and uncomplicated work best for this activity) and make sure that you will not be distracted for at least 20 minutes. Get very comfortable and relaxed. You may even want to put on a visualization tape or some relaxing music or meditate if you are used to doing that. Then allow yourself to feel whatever you are feeling. Do not think about it—just feel. Stay inside yourself and stay with these feelings as you pick up your crayon, marker, colored pencils, or paint and begin to express these feelings on paper. Reserve judgment about what you are producing and do not let your mind engage in thoughts about it. Stay focused in the present and in the experience of expression. Allow yourself to use the materials any way that feels right. It is the process of expression that counts, not the result. Later, you might want to try dialoguing with your picture. You might ask: Why do you feel this way? What do you need? How can I help?

This reminds me of another activity, which can be equally releasing: writing your feelings. When I was just a child, I discovered the power of putting feelings into words myself by sitting down one day after school and writing my angry feelings in a letter to a friend who had hurt my feelings earlier that day. I was going to give her that letter, but I found that after I wrote it, I felt fine and no longer needed to. This was such a simple activity and yet so powerful! There are many good books on the market that explain how journaling (i.e. writing in a journal) can be used to work with feelings, explore inner motivations and needs, and access creativity and the Higher Self. Several are listed in the bibliography.

Drawing can also be a form of meditation by bringing all your awareness to what you are making. Involving yourself totally in the creative process relaxes you, quiets your mind, makes room for your intuition, and allows messages from your Higher Self to come forward. This activity also gives you prac- tice in staying in the present. Here is how to use art for medita- tion:

Relax and quiet yourself, using music, a visualization tape, deep breathing, progressive relaxation, or meditation. When you are ready, allow your hand to move spontaneously. It should feel like the picture is just drawing itself; some even call this Automatic Drawing. (Many recommend using the nondominant hand for this as well as for any art therapy work.) Remain focused on the paper and what you are creating. Whenever your mind wanders, just bring it back to the activity. Don't plan what you will draw, just let it flow, and involve yourself totally in the experience of the colors and designs you are making.

Just as clairvoyants sometimes receive information from other realms in the form of visual symbols, we too can receive messages from our soul in the form of visual symbols. Images are released from the superconscious and subconscious minds into the conscious mind continually while we are awake. Most of the time, we miss them. Art provides a way of capturing them, validating them, and deciphering them. These messages can provide information useful in our healing and growth.

Art Activities

What follows are some ideas for using art to contact and express the Self, which is healing to every aspect of ourselves, not only to our emotions. Be sure to allow at least 20 minutes of uninterrupted time for each experience. A calm, quiet atmosphere and the absence of distractions is important in being able to involve yourself as completely as you need to. You might

---

Art is Healing

♥ It is a means of discovering, acknowledging, accepting and expressing feelings.

♥ It is a means of releasing unconscious material, including feelings, from the unconscious.

♥ It is a means of meditating and learning to be in the present.

♥ It is a means of receiving messages from our Higher Self.

---

want to put on some meditative music in the background to help you alter your consciousness and set the mood. Be sure you have all the art supplies you need within reach. Have a brief period of meditation prior to it to still the mind.

One purpose of these experiences is to allow Spirit to communicate its joy, love, and upliftment through you. By aligning yourself with these positive emotions and allowing yourself to be a vehicle for manifesting them in the world, you are cleansed by them and your creations will have a similar impact on others. Your technical skills or even the quality and type of materials you use have little to do with the effect of this experience on you or others.

Producing something this way is an act of surrender. You are allowing yourself to be a vehicle for whatever wants to be expressed through you. It may be that what wants to be expressed is not all sweetness and light but intensity and darkness. The dark is a foil for the light and an equally important principle in our experience. So, try not to be judgmental or have any expectations about your creations.

What will come through you depends on what Spirit wants to communicate through you and to you. Through the experience of creating, you will discover something about yourself or about life that hadn't entered your awareness before. Whether others have the same insight when they view it is unimportant; they may or may not. Sometimes Spirit uses the symbols in someone's art work to evoke an entirely different insight in someone else. You never know what purpose your creations may serve for others; that is not in your hands.

Even if you do not choose to share what you create with others (and you may not want to, since using art this way is very personal) or preserve what you create, you will have benefitted from the process of creation. Creating always holds something special, something very personal, for the creator.

Activity 1: Manifesting an Ideal

Choose an ideal you wish to express or a quality you would like to instill. It could be love, peace, hope, beauty, truth, devotion, courage, perseverance, patience, acceptance, serenity, humor, lightheartedness, joy, playfulness, humility, strength, inspiration, or anything you wish to manifest more strongly in the world either personally or for the good of humankind. Know that the act you are about to partake in has real power on spiritual levels to change you and to change the world.

Find a comfortable and quiet place. Put on appropriate music, something that fits the ideal you wish to evoke. Relax and allow yourself to feel the feelings that accompany this ideal. Feel those feelings in every part of your being. Allow any images to come to mind that represent that ideal. Then, when you are ready, keeping as mentally still as possible, begin to express through your chosen medium whatever you feel as you focus on the ideal or quality. It might be helpful to use your nondominant hand for this. The nondominant hand (the left hand of a right-handed person) is controlled by the right hemisphere of the brain, which is involved in emotional expression and non-verbal, visual, creative, and intuitive processes. Don't be concerned about what you are producing. Allow yourself to move naturally and effortlessly, without thought and without judgment. The more often you do this activity, the easier it will be to allow Spirit to express itself through you.

Activity 2: Obtaining Guidance

Formulate a question in your mind that you would like answered, similar to one you would ask a divinatory tool or on a guided visualization. You might ask: What do I need now to heal myself? What is at the root of this problem? How can I facilitate my growth? What is this symptom trying to tell me? What is missing in my life? or What do I need? Affirm your desire to receive an answer to this question, whatever it may be. Also affirm your belief that an answer is obtainable through this means. Affirm your power to know yourself, to know what is best for you. The answers truly are within you.

Take time to relax completely before drawing your answer. Put on music that helps you relax and turn within. Do not let your mind wander while you are relaxing. Try to feel your question. Is it located in any particular part of your body? Pay attention to all your inward sensations. Then, when you are ready, begin expressing yourself through your chosen medium freely. Do not analyze the process or the results. Pay attention to how you feel as you are creating; that will help you understand your answer. Stay with this process until it feels complete. If you didn't receive an insight during this process, repeat it sometime or meditate on or dialogue with what you have created.

Activity 3: Evoking Positive Feelings

Think of a time in your life when you felt most happy, most

content and at peace with life. Really get into those feelings again. Play some relaxing music, lie back, and re-create that time in your mind. When you feel ready, express how you felt then through your chosen medium. Express yourself freely and without interruption from your thoughts. Just stay focused in the process. Realigning with Spirit will become very natural as this exercise is repeated.

Peace and acceptance are always available whether or not your life is running smoothly. What is going on in your life may interfere with your sense of peace, acceptance, and love of God, but these positive feelings are always available if you don't block them. It's just that when our lives are chaotic, challenging, or not going as we would like them, we often lose our connection with Spirit and the peace that connection provides. This activity shows you that peace can be reinstated whenever you call upon it—whenever you invoke it. You are meant to live in peace and acceptance always. So, claim your right to this, and meditate on your creative product to re-experience this state any time you wish to.

Activity 4: Communicating with Spirit

Create an opportunity for Spirit to express whatever it will through you through your chosen medium. Affirm your openness and willingness to be a channel for Spirit. Relax very deeply and do whatever is necessary to get into a meditative state. When you are fully relaxed and centered within yourself, allow whatever comes to you to be expressed through your chosen medium. Refrain from all judgment, analysis, or thought. When the process feels complete, give thanks to Spirit for its message. Afterwards, you might want to meditate on what you have created or dialogue with it to determine its meaning for you.

Activity 5: Contacting Your Inner Healer

This activity is from *The Picture of Health*:

Quiet yourself and turn within. Meditate on the aspect of yourself that is the Inner Healer. Using your nondominant hand, have your Inner Healer draw itself. Now have a dialogue with your Inner Healer either in writing or out loud. Ask your

Inner Healer questions about whatever is bothering you and needs healing. The value of this experience is not only in the information you receive but in affirming your belief in an Inner Healer. This belief alone is potentially healing.

This same process can be done with your Inner Child, that part of you that is still a vulnerable child with emotional needs that are not always met or whose emotional needs may not have been met in the past.

CHAPTER 5 NOTES

1. Kay Ortmans, *"Reminders from Well-Springs"* booklet (San Francisco: Well-Springs Foundation, 1987), p. 13.

2. From *"Discovery on the Wing"* pamphlet by Kay Ortmans.

3. Sara Lonsdale and Kay Ortmans, *Let Go to Music, Rebound to Life* (San Francisco: Well-Springs Foundation, 1987), p. 10.

4. Ibid., p. 15.

5. Ibid., p. 11.

6. Kay Ortmans, *"Reminders from Well-Springs"* booklet (San Francisco: Well-Springs Foundation, 1987), p. 18.

7. Pir Hazrat Inayat Khan, *"Healing with Sound and Music,"* *Music: Physician for Times to Come*, ed. Don Campbell (Wheaton, Ill.: Theosophical Publishing House, 1991), p. 323.

8. Laeh Maggie Garfield, *Sound Medicine: Healing with Music, Voice, and Song* (Berkeley, Calif.: Celestial Arts, 1987), p. 87.

9. Andrew Watson and Nevill Drury, *Healing Music* (England: Prism Press, 1987), p.10.

10. Tim Wilson, *"Chant: "The Healing Power of Voice and Ear,"* *Music: Physician for Times to Come*, ed. Don Campbell (Wheaton, Ill.: The Theosophical Publishing House, 1991).

11. Cathie E. Guzetta, *"Music Therapy: Nursing the Music of the Soul," Music: Physician for Times to Come*, ed. Don Campbell (Wheaton Ill.: The Theosophical Publishing House, 1991), p. 153.

12. Laeh Maggie Garfield, *Sound Medicine: Healing with Music, Voice, and Song* (Berkeley, Calif.: Celestial Arts, 1987.), p. 8.

13. Ibid., p. 43-44.
14. Olivea Dewhurst-Maddock, *The Book of Sound Therapy* (New York: Simon & Schuster, 1993), p. 89.

15. Miriam Therese Winter, *"Music, the Way Home," Music: Physician for Times to Come*, ed. Don Campbell (Wheaton Ill.: The Theosophical Publishing House, 1991), p. 259-260.

CHAPTER 5 SOURCES

Campbell, Don, ed. *Music: Physician for Times to Come.* Wheaton, Ill.: Theosophical Publishing House, 1991.

Capacchione, Lucia. *The Picture of Health: Healing Your Life with Art.* Santa Monica, Calif.: Hay House, 1990.

Dewhurst-Maddock, Olivea. *The Book of Sound Therapy: Heal Yourself with Music and Voice.* New York: Simon & Schuster, 1993.

Garfield, Laeh Maggie. *Sound Medicine: Healing with Music, Voice, and Song.* Berkeley, Calif.: Celestial Arts, 1987.

Lonsdale, Sara and Kay Ortmans. *Let Go to Music, Rebound to Life.* San Francisco: Well-Springs Foundation, 1987.

Ortmans, Kay. *"Reminders from Well-Springs"* booklet. San Francisco: Well-Springs Foundation, 1987.

Watson, Andrew and Nevill Drury. *Healing Music: The Harmonic Path to Inner Wholeness*. Garden City Park, N.Y.: Avery Publishing Group, 1987.

CHAPTER 5 SUGGESTED READING

Music

Andrews, Ted. *Sacred Sounds: Transformation Through Music and Word*. St. Paul: Llewellyn, 1992.

Bonny, Helen and Louis Savary. *Music and Your Mind: Listening with a New Consciousness*. New York: Harper & Row, 1973.

Campbell, Don, ed. *Music and Miracles*. Wheaton, Ill.: The Theosophical Publishing House, 1992.

Drury, Nevill. *Music for Inner Space*. San Leandro, CA: Prism Press, 1985.

Halpern, Steven and Louis Savary. *Sound Health: The Music and Sounds that Make Us Whole*. San Francisco: Harper & Row, 1985.

Halpern, Steven and Louis Savary. *Tuning the Human Instrument*. Belmont, Calif.: Spectrum Research Institute, 1978.

Hamel, Peter Michael. *Through Music to the Self*. Boulder, Colorado: Shambhala, 1979.

Khan, Hazrat Inayat. *The Music of Life*. Lebanon Spring, N.Y.: The Sufi Order, 1983.

Art

Capacchione, Lucia and Elizabeth Johnson and James Strohecker. *Lighten Up Your Body, Lighten Up Your Life*. North Hollywood: Newcastle, 1990.

Capacchione, Lucia. *The Picture of Health: Healing Your Life with Art*. Santa Monica, Calif.: Hay House, 1990.

Fincher, Susanne, F. *Creating Mandalas for Insight, Healing, and Self-Expression*. Boston: Shambhala, 1991.

Journaling

Capacchione, Lucia. *The Power of Your Other Hand*. North Hollywood: Newcastle, 1988. (Also uses art.)

Capacchione, Lucia. *The Creative Journal*. North Hollywood: Newcastle, 1989. (Also uses art.)

Capacchione, Lucia. *The Well-Being Journal*. North Hollywood: Newcastle, 1989. (Also uses art.)

Chapman, Joyce. *Journaling for Joy: Writing Your Way to Personal Growth and Freedom*. North Hollywood: Newcastle, 1991.

Progoff, Ira, M.D. *At a Journal Workshop: Writing to Access the Power of the Unconscious and Evoke Creative Ability*. Los Angeles: Jeremy P. Tarcher, 1992.

MOVEMENT RESOURCES

Information about workshops and Well-Springs; and a catalog listing audio cassette tapes for movement, cassettes for children, and video tapes about the program (for home or school use) can be obtained from:

Well-Springs Foundation, Ltd.
21 North Prospect Ave.
Madison, WI 53705
(608) 233-5188

Let Go to Music, Rebound to Life by Sara Lonsdale and Kay Ortmans can be obtained from the above address for $10.00 plus shipping and handling. Although this is a teacher's training manual for the Well-Springs Program, it has an excellent and extensive list of classical music selections suitable for movement activities, making it a valuable resource for anyone interested in using music and movement for healing.

CLASSICAL MUSIC SUGGESTIONS

Movement

Vaughn-Williams, *Folk Suite*
Handel, *Water Music*

Gentle

Franck, *Symphony in B minor*
Rachmaninoff, *Piano Concerto #3*

Energy

Brahms, *Piano Concerto #1*
Brahms, *Piano Quintet*
Mozart, *Symphonies #38 and 39*

Deep Response

Rachmaninoff, *Isle of the Dead*
Mahler, *Symphony #2, Resurrection*

Higher Consciousness

Puccini, *Mass*
Allegri, *Miserere*
Faure, *Collection*
Brahms *Requiem*

These recordings are stocked by Tower Records, 2727 S. El Camino Real, San Mateo, CA 94403. Phone: (415) 570-4600. You must contact Barry Guerrero, Classical Department. Failing that, contact Hobart at (415) 368-7644 and he will give directions.

(This list courtesy of Kay Ortmans and reprinted with her permission)

SUGGESTED MUSIC

Berhardt, Patrick. *Atlantis Angelis.* Shining Star Music.

Berhardt, Patrick. *Solaris Universalis.* Shining Star Music.

Bhava. *Vajra Sattva.* Clear Light Music.

Gass, Robert. *Om Namaha Shivaya.* Spring Hill Music.

Gass, Robert.. *Shri Ram.* Spring Hill Music.

Halpern, Steven. *Spectrum Suite.* Halpern Sounds.

Jaya. *Baba's Garden.* Blackburnian Records.

Jaya. *Bring Down the Light.* Blackburnian Records.

Jaya. *Dance in Ecstasy.* Blackburnian Records.

Jaya. *Sacred Streams.* Blackburnian Records.

Jaya. *Shelter for Your Heart.* Blackburnian Records.

Jaya. *Songs to Ammachi.* Blackburnian Records.

Kitaro. *Silk Road.* Geffen Records.

Kitaro. *The Light of the Spirit.* Geffen Records.

Shakti, Nada. *Samadhi.* Shining Star Music.

(no artist listed:)

I Will Sing Thy Name. Self-Realization Fellowship.

Jai Ma Kirtan. Sri Rama Publishing.

Song Divine: Kiirtan from Anandapalli. Inner Song.

Song Divine 2: Kiirtan from Anandapalli. Inner Song.

Songs of the Lord's Love. Invincible Records.

Sri Ram Kirtan. Sri Rama Publishing.

RESOURCES FOR MUSIC TAPES

Aura Communications, P.O. Box 5256, San Diego, CA 92105.

Blackburnian Records, 509 W.Olin Ave., Madison, WI 53715.

Bodymind Systems, 910 Dakota Dr., Temple, TX 76501.

Clear Light Music, Star Route, Box 174, Hana, Maui, HI 96713.

Fortuna Records, 11 Kavon Ct., Novato, CA 94947.

Halpern Sounds, 1775 Old County Rd., #9, Belmont, CA 94002.

Inner Guidance System, GWYNEDD, Plaza 2, Suite 301, Springhouse, PA 19477.

Inner Song, 4095 Jackdaw, San Diego, CA 92103.

Invincible Records, P.O. Box 13054, Phoenix, AZ 85002.

Mystical Rose Books and Tapes, P.O. Box 38, Malibu, CA 90265.

Narada Distributing, 1804 E. North Ave., Milwaukee, WI 53202

Self-Realization Fellowship. 3880 San Rafael Ave., Los Angeles, CA 90065.

Shining Star Music, 417 Tamal Plaza, Corte Madera, CA 94925.

Sound of Light, Box 1244, Boulder, CO 80306.

Source Distributing and New Age Co-Op, P.O. Box 1207, Carmel Valley, CA 93924.

Sources Cassette, Dept. 99, P.O. Box W, Stanford, CA 94305.

Spring Hill Music, P.O. Box 800, Boulder, CO 80306

Sri Rama Publishing, Box 2550, Santa Cruz, CA 95063.

Valley of the Sun Publishing, P.O. Box 38, Malibu, CA 90265.

CHAPTER 6
Astrology and Other Esoteric Tools

Astrology

Astrology is misunderstood. This is partly the fault of the media, but astrologers who write sun sign columns and forecasts for newspapers and magazines must take some responsibility too. By catering to the public's desire for forecasting, or perhaps just to its desire to be entertained, a few astrologers have made a name for themselves at astrology's expense. Today, serious astrologers are having difficulty living down the legacy of sun sign columns. Although some information about the astrological signs is offered in these columns and they do increase the public's awareness of astrology, what is offered is too superficial and general to be meaningful, but just enough to give discriminating minds cause to dismiss astrology as a serious science. Most who read these columns don't take them seriously either but read them as entertainment. The few who do take them seriously are often misled by them.

Astrology is complex; it is the most complex of the esoteric tools and requires years of study and experience before its secrets are unlocked. It is interesting that those most opposed to it often know the least about it. But, here again, the problem lies not only in the public's ignorance of astrology, but also with astrologers themselves. Some who practice it do not acquire the experience, knowledge, intuition, and counseling skills needed to do it well. Because licensing is not required of astrologers and few formal courses of instruction exist, astrologers are not always adequately trained. Thus, poor performance by astrologers also reflects badly on astrology.

Astrology is difficult for many to believe in not only for these reasons but because it is so irrational. How can it be true? It doesn't seem possible that the moment of our birth could influence (or reflect) our personality, talents, trials, and goals. It goes against reason. And yet, there will always be things we cannot explain, since the universe is far more intricate and vast than our minds at this stage in our evolution can grasp. The fact that astrology works demonstrates to me that there are things beyond my comprehension and, moreover, that the intelligence behind it all is awesome.

The sense of awe that astrology inspires in me is one of the things I appreciate most about it. I appreciate the glimpse it gives me into the Mind of God and the miracle of life. If astrology is true, what does this mean? To me, it means that there is an unimaginable Intelligence at work and this Intelligence has a plan of which we are all a part. The astrological birth chart is the symbolic representation of each person's unique plan. Astrologers have learned to read this plan's unfolding over time through the transits and the progressions.

The astrological birth chart, or horoscope, is a picture of the skies as seen from earth at the moment of birth. It pictures the patterns the planets formed in the sky at birth. Someone born at a particular moment in time is a reflection of those patterns, which can be interpreted by reading the chart. Thus, astrology is a symbolic language that allows us to know what energies characterize someone.

These energies do not compel us to do anything, but they do create drives, needs, and tendencies. So, an astrologer cannot predict how someone will behave or what choices he or she will make, but the astrologer can identify a person's talents, potentials, psychological needs, and psychological issues. The chart also pictures a person's spiritual lessons and goals.

There are different kinds of astrologers. You will want to find one who specializes in the area of your inquiry. There are karmic astrologers for those wanting reincarnational or spiritual insight, psychological or humanistic astrologers for those interested in self-awareness and emotional healing, financial astrologers for those wanting investment advice, and medical astrologers for those with health problems. Some also specialize in vocational guidance, although this is something most astrologers are equipped to give.

All astrologers will speak to you about your transits and progressions, or what is going on now in terms of your chart. Some will attempt to make specific predictions based on your transits and progressions. But unless someone is psychic or very lucky it is extremely difficult to make specific predictions, and most good astrologers won't even try. Even if an astrologer could make accurate predictions, this practice is questionable. Predicting the future is disempowering. It leaves us feeling that we are not in control of our lives, that our lives are fated. In truth, our lives are largely created by our choices.

Transits and progressions are best used to help us understand our growth and experiences from a higher perspective. Through the analysis of transits and progressions, the lessons we are learning at a particular time can be identified. So, the purpose of transits and progressions is to help us understand what we are already experiencing, not to try to determine what will happen to us. When used this way, astrology is a powerful tool for self-awareness and growth. It helps us see that our experiences are part of a process of growth, not just meaningless events. Life is not meaningless, and astrology holds the key to unlocking the meaning of our life and experiences.

A good astrologer will not tell you what to do any more than a good psychotherapist would. A good astrologer supplies information to help you make the most satisfying choices. Astrology, by so clearly picturing what we need to feel happy, fulfilled, and whole, is perfectly suited to helping us examine and explore ways to get our basic psychological needs met.

The chart pictures our psychological needs, which relate to our spiritual needs. Essentially, by fulfilling our psychological needs, we are assured of fulfilling our spiritual needs. This is why feelings are so important: They tell us of our psychological and spiritual needs. When these needs are not being met, anger, resentment, sadness, depression, or guilt arise. The chart informs us of our psychological needs so that we can take steps to meet them and avoid these unpleasant feelings as much as possible.

Our psychological needs are represented by the planets and can be thought of as subpersonalities within us, each with its own needs. For instance, we may have a subpersonality symbolized by the moon in Cancer, who has a need for security, home, family, and intimate relationships. We may have another subpersonality symbolized by the sun in Aquarius, who has a need for freedom, invention, humanitarian service, and involvement with many different people. Obviously, there will be times when the needs of both these subpersonalities will not be able to be met, and one will have to submit to the other or find a way of compromising.

If we didn't have numerous conflicting drives within us, life would be simpler, but these conflicts provide the challenges that evolve us, strengthen us, and develop our resources. Thus, these conflicts serve a purpose and can function in our favor once we become aware of them and learn to make conscious choices in meeting their needs.

The subpersonalities within the psyche are a little like the

The Psychological Needs of the Signs

ARIES: need for freedom, independence, initiative, discovery, self-assertion, and leadership.

TAURUS: need for sensual pleasures, comfort, security, and productivity.

GEMINI: need to know, to communicate, to teach, to move about, and to make contact with people and the environment.

CANCER: need for roots, family, home, community, and security. Need to give and receive nurturing.

LEO: need for ego expansion, independence, recognition, authority, admiration, leadership, self-expression, creativity, and love.

VIRGO: need to be efficient and useful, to serve, to analyze, to organize, and to do things well.

LIBRA: need for partnership, beauty, balance, justice, harmony, and peace.

SCORPIO: need for self-mastery, power, control, self-transformation, intimacy, hidden knowledge, and psychological understanding.

SAGITTARIUS: need for meaning, freedom, independence, growth, understanding, a philosophy, travel, and exploration.

CAPRICORN: need for structure, control, leadership, responsibility, achievement, power, recognition, status, and security.

AQUARIUS: need for egalitarian relationships, freedom, independence, group involvement, friendship, community, and individualism. Need to invent and to reform society.

PISCES: need for transcendence, escape, spirituality, beauty, ideal love, emotional closeness, serenity, and privacy. Need to serve.

instruments in an orchestra. Each is important to the whole and meant to work in harmony with the whole. When they don't, the result is discordant and unpleasant. Someone who gains awareness of the different instruments can become the conductor, the master of his or her psyche. The conductor's job is to create harmony in the orchestra. The conductor oversees the whole, indicates when one instrument is meant to play and another remain silent, and tells each instrument how loud to play and with what kind of expression.

The work of therapy is to define and develop this conductor; the work of astrology is to name the orchestra members. In a sense, all healing works to create and perfect the conductor. The difference between holistic healing and other types of treatment is who is assumed to be the conductor. Holistic healing assumes this conductor is the Higher Self, while more traditional therapies may be satisfied with the ego as conductor.

To benefit from an astrological reading, it is not necessary to know anything about astrology. However, to work with your subpersonalities further on your own for purposes of healing, you will need a grasp of the twelve signs of the zodiac, or at least the ones prominent in your chart. The twelve signs are an emotional alphabet. They represent twelve primary human needs or drives. Although these twelve needs or drives are present in everyone to some extent, each or us has a unique combination of them.

Once you have learned something about your subpersonalities and their needs from a professional astrologer, and with some additional help from astrology books (see the bibliography at the end of this chapter), there are a number of things you can do to heal the discordant, poorly functioning, or repressed parts of yourself. The activities that follow can be done alone, but they also can be fun, informative, and healing when done with others. The potential for healing is often greater in groups because of the combined energy of the members, their insights, and their commitment to keeping the work focused. Two or more people joining together for healing sends a clear call to Spirit, which Spirit answers by bestowing intuitive insights and healing energy, and by spurring others on intuitively to provide the help needed.

Perhaps one of the easiest and most useful ways of working with your chart by yourself is to have a written or spoken dialogue with one of the planets in your chart, one whose expression you would like to improve upon. Often one or more of our subpersonalities is denied, judged, or impoverished and needs our understanding and attention. When left unattended to, it may act compulsively and unconsciously, and sabotage our happiness and success.

A subpersonality becomes problematic for many reasons. We may have had a parent who did not like this part of ourselves, we may have another subpersonality in direct conflict with it, or we may have mishandled this energy in previous lifetimes or had little experience with it before this lifetime. Whatever the reason, our most troublesome subpersonalities are discordant notes in our orchestra and will continue to create dissonance within us until they are acknowledged and accepted, and their needs are met. Once we allow them to "live," they often have gifts to offer us.

Gestalt Therapy, which was developed by Fritz Perls, recognizes, along with many other therapies, the importance of acknowledging, accepting, and meeting the needs of every part of ourselves—all our subpersonalities. Gestalt Therapy uses certain techniques for working with subpersonalities, most notably the empty chair technique. This technique—which consists of dialoguing with a subpersonality, who is supposedly sitting in a chair across from us—is useful in working with the subpersonalities identified by our astrological chart. It can be used alone or in groups. It also can be done in writing instead of spoken aloud.

To use the empty chair technique by yourself to dialogue with a malfunctioning, repressed, or unhappy part of yourself, have the troubled subpersonality sit in a chair across from you and begin a conversation with it. Tell it how you feel about it and the problems it has created. Then ask it how it feels, why it is unhappy, what it wants, what it suggests you do to get its needs met, and what gifts it has to offer. Then, switch chairs and play the part of the subpersonality and answer with whatever comes to mind. Dialogue back and forth until you understand the role this subpersonality is playing in your life. Through dialogue, you will come to realize that this subpersonality is only troublesome because it is neglected. With a few concessions, it is likely to behave better. Usually these concessions are made in the course of the dialogue.

This may seem fanciful; however, like imagery, past-life

Working with your Subpersonalities

★ Visualize the positive qualities of the subpersonality you hope to develop (i.e. the positive qualities of the sign related to that subpersonality) and feel what it would be like to express those qualities. Feel this emotionally and bodily. Doing this in a light trance will increase its effectiveness.

You may want to tape record an induction and a description of an ideal version of this subpersonality so that you can listen to it as many times as you need to. Be sure to phrase the visualization in the first person. For example, to transform negative Aries energy into positive Aries energy, you might begin like this: "I am full of energy, strength, courage, and drive. My strength is focused and applied with precision to my goals. . . ." Essentially, this tape will be affirmations to counteract the negative qualities of your subpersonality and strengthen the positive ones. The act of creating a tape is, in itself, healing because of the effort involved and the intent for healing it conveys.

Before you can make a tape, you may need to do some self-analysis to understand how this subpersonality is operating negatively and how you want it to operate in the future. To help you in your self-analysis, you might want to try the next two activities:

★ Meditate on this subpersonality by sitting quietly with eyes closed and mind stilled and focused on the astrological symbol for that subpersonality. Allow any images to come to mind. Feel what it feels like to be this subpersonality so that you can understand it better. Now, erase this image in your mind, like erasing a blackboard, and summon up the positive qualities of this subpersonality you hope to develop.

★ Draw your subpersonality. This will help you get in touch with this energy so that you understand it better. Dialogue with it. Once you have done this, draw a new, improved version of this subpersonality and dialogue with it. This will help you feel what the transformed subpersonality will feel like and establish it in your consciousness. By drawing what you want it to be like, you are creating a model for it, which helps bring it into manifestation. But more than this, the act

(cont'd. next page)

of drawing—or working with a subpersonality in any of the suggested ways—is a statement of your desire to heal it, and this elicits Spirit's help.

★ Cut out pictures from magazines and make a collage illustrating the positive attributes of the planetary energy you want to improve on or express more freely. This is a kind of treasure map. For instance, if you want to develop the positive qualities of your Cancer sun, pictures of puppies, babies, and homey scenes could evoke your Cancer sun's warmth and nurturing. Meditate on these images. Place this collage on the refrigerator or some other prominent place in your home where you will see it often. Seeing these images repeatedly and reinforcing them with affirmations of how you want to be will help you express those positive qualities in the world.

★ Find music that reflects the planetary energy you wish to integrate or express more positively. This music can just be listened to or it can accompany any visualization work you do or it can be danced to (with props or masks for extra fun). It also can be used to inspire you as you draw this planetary energy. Barbara Schermer, the author of a book about astro-drama, suggests using Gustav Holst's "*The Planets*," which is a symphonic suite in seven movements exemplifying Mars, Venus, Mercury, Jupiter, Saturn, Uranus, and Neptune. But finding your own music for a particular planetary energy may be even more effective because of the effort and personal involvement it entails.

regression, and other techniques that work with the unconscious, this technique has a powerful potential for healing. It not only provides insight into the problems and needs of the subpersonality, it actually helps heal and integrate it into the rest of the personality. Just attending to this part by listening to it deepens your relationship to it and gives it a whole new relationship to the psyche. It is no longer a second-class citizen and it begins to act more appropriately and in harmony with the other energies.

The empty chair technique also can be used with two subpersonalities that are in conflict. This is done by placing two chairs opposite each other and carrying out a dialogue by switching back and forth from one chair to the other as you take each part. One subpersonality should start out by saying how it feels and what it needs. Then the other subpersonality responds, expressing its feelings and needs. The dialogue continues until a compromise or resolution is reached. Here is an example of this:

Gemini Moon: I am so tired of staying in the house I could scream. I need to get out, go places, see the world, talk to people! How can you stand being shut in all day writing at a computer? I've had it!

Pisces Sun: It's nice and quiet here. Nobody bothers us. I get to think and dream and be creative. What are you complaining about, you like ideas don't you?

Gemini Moon: Yes, I like ideas, but I'd like to listen to someone else's ideas for a change. I'm tired of thinking of the same subject. I want to think about something else.

Pisces Sun: Not yet. I'm right in the middle of an idea that I need to get down.

Gemini Moon: No way. We're doing something else now! Let's drive downtown and pick up that book we ordered.

Pisces Sun: No. I'm not in the mood for crowds. Let's go for a walk in the woods instead.

Gemini Moon: Oh, all right. That's better than nothing. At least we'll get out. But tomorrow night can we go to a movie?

Pisces Sun It's a deal; movies are a great escape!

The conflict between a Pisces sun and a Gemini moon can be a major one. Any time someone's sun and moon sign are very different, a major conflict is likely. Once you get to know your chart's themes and the twelve signs, you will be able to recognize your inner conflicts and how they play out in your psyche. The above dialogue turned out favorably, because a

compromise was found; but too often our conflicting subpersonalities either become stalemated or one is repressed,
expressed inappropriately, or projected. Holding dialogues
between our conflicting subpersonalities gets the issues out in
the open so that steps can be taken to resolve the conflict.

Dialogues can even be carried out between more than two
subpersonalities. For instance, you could have other members
of your psychic family give you their input on the conflict
between two subpersonalities. Or, you could have several
subpersonalities respond to a certain issue in turn, which would
be like holding a meeting between the members of your
psychic family. [1] When working with several subpersonalities,
instead of just using chairs to identify each one, you might want

---

Using Astrology in Groups for Healing

♦ The group can observe each others' empty chair
dialogues and offer their insights after each one.

♦ People from the group can take turns playing the part
of the subpersonality for each other.

♦ Two members of the group may enact someone in
the group's conflicting subpersonalities, while that
person looks on. By watching others act out our internal
conflicts, we might gain new insights into how our
conflicting energies operate and how we can better
handle them. We also might acquire more of a sense of
humor about this conflict, which can be healing. Humor
gives us some distance from the conflict and consequently space to heal it.

♦ An entire chart can be enacted by a group if there are
at least ten people in the group with a good knowledge
of astrology. Barbara Schermer, in her book *Astrology
Alive!*, gives suggestions for how this can be done.

---

to use masks or other props to help you maintain the character of that subpersonality. For example, you might put on a policeman's hat when sitting in the Capricorn subpersonality's chair or an outrageous wig when playing the part of your outrageous Aquarius subpersonality.

Some psychotherapists are using astrology this way in group work as one tool in their therapeutic toolbox. They are either conversant in astrology themselves or they join forces with an astrologer.

Astrodrama, or the enacting of a horoscope or parts of a horoscope, is one way of experiencing our planetary energies. It takes astrology out of the realm of the intellect and gets our body, senses, and emotions involved. In dramatizing our energies, we externalize the internal—we make the unconscious conscious—which is a big step in healing. The dramatization goes further, however, in also offering a means for healing the wounded parts of ourselves and integrating our internal conflicts.

Astrodrama also can increase our compassion for ourselves and the various parts of ourselves, for we begin to see our subpersonalities as entities with a life of their own and with legitimate needs. We realize these parts of ourselves do not have to be our adversaries: We can make peace with them. Furthermore, making peace with ourselves extends to our relationships, for in learning to be more compassionate with ourselves, we learn to be more compassionate with others.

Astrodrama can be fun and informative. However, when it becomes more like psychodrama, that is, when it is used in a group as a means of working through negative emotions and early childhood issues, it should be guided by skilled professionals. Astrodrama used this way can elicit deep feelings, which may need additional support to work through. Group work also can be a way of learning astrology for those interested in tackling this.

If you find that you are angry at or unable to dialogue with a certain planetary energy, you may have been denying or repressing it. These energies will be especially important to work with, so don't give up too easily. [2]

Choosing an Astrologer

If understanding our chart was easy, we would all be very wise. But charts are not easy to interpret; in-depth readings require years of training and experience. And although some of my fellow astrologers disagree, I believe a good reading also depends on good counseling skills. Certainly the experience of a reading with an astrologer trained in counseling would be different than a reading with an astrologer without this training, even if the information was not very different. An astrological reading is much more than information-giving, whether it acknowledges this or not. What information is given, how it is given, and what information is withheld are all crucial in determining whether that reading will be healing or not. Astrology is essentially a counseling profession.

Astrology is a high calling. Astrologers are given a great deal of power by clients and it is in everyone's best interest that this power is used wisely. You as a consumer have no say in how astrology is practiced or who practices it, but you have every say in choosing an astrologer. On the following page are some guidelines to help you.

A session with a professional astrologer will cost you much more than just a computer-generated analysis, however. Don't be deceived into thinking that you can get a good astrological reading from a computer or otherwise for $20, $30 or even $40. When you see prices like these, you can be sure there is no personalized work involved. The other possibility is that the astrologer is just starting out. As with so many things, you get what you pay for (and sometimes not even that). You will have to pay anywhere from $60—$150 and sometimes more for a reading from a professional astrologer. Astrologers who charge more than this are not necessarily better than ones who charge the going rate; they just have made a name for themselves and are in demand.

Some astrologers, both good and bad, advertise, but many good ones do not advertise at all. Word of mouth is all some astrologers need to stay busy. So, the best astrologers are not necessarily the ones advertising. A good way to find an astrologer is through a recommendation from someone you trust or a referral from a holistic health care professional. Acupuncturists, massage therapists, transpersonal psychotherapists, naturopaths, doctors of homeopathy, Rolfers, and chiropractors often know of good astrologers. Most metaphysical bookstores have the names of local

Choosing an Astrologer

★ Find out the astrologer's philosophy, approach, background, experience, and credentials. How did he or she learn astrology? For how long and how intensively did he or she study before becoming a professional astrologer? How long has he or she been practicing professionally? Is this a full or part-time practice, a hobby, or something done in addition to another career?

★ Is the astrologer willing to give you references? Don't be afraid to ask for references if you don't know anyone else who has gone to that astrologer. Not everyone who advertises is qualified; anyone can call himself or herself an astrologer.

★ Find out what the astrologer is offering. Some astrologers sell computer-generated analyses, handwritten analyses, or taped readings with no face-to-face session at all. These are only so helpful unless they are followed up by a session. Without knowing something about you and having an opportunity to meet you and ask you questions, even the best astrologer can offer only general information.

astrologers also, but they may not know who to recommend. Some cities have alternative health care directories, but they usually cannot be counted on to screen those listed. They are primarily vehicles for advertising.

One last note about the astrological reading: Astrologers and others who use esoteric tools often use what you tell them about yourself to guide them in their interpretation. Without knowing how you are expressing the energies of your chart, it can be hard for an astrologer to give you an insightful and relevant reading, although even general psychological information may be helpful. Still, much more can be obtained when the counselor knows something about you.

Because of this, if you go to an astrologer or esoteric counselor, be prepared to give him or her background information about yourself and the subject of your inquiry. Many people refrain from telling astrologers or esoteric counselors anything about themselves, because they expect them to already know what they need through their tools or intuitive gifts. Although people who are psychically or intuitively developed often can address your questions adequately without knowing anything about you, the more information they have, the more they can fit their impressions to your specific situation and help you with it.

Be clear about why you want a reading. If you are just going to see if astrology works, why waste your time and money? Astrology and other esoteric tools work when they are used by a skilled, intuitive practitioner. If you have any doubts about someone's skills, don't go to that individual. Find someone who has been highly recommended, and then work with him or her as you would with any counselor. Don't go into a session looking for ways to trip up the counselor. Instead, try to help the counselor help you.

Astrology is such an important tool for psycho-spiritual understanding and healing. Any efforts you make to find a good astrologer and understand your chart will be well worthwhile.

Other Esoteric Tools

Esoteric tools—astrology, palmistry, numerology, the Tarot, the Runes, and the *I Ching*—are a way that those without psychic gifts can get insight into the soul's plan. There are others, but many of them are versions of these. *Native American Medicine Cards*, for example, are a version of the Tarot. I am including the Runes, the *I Ching*, and the Tarot under esoteric tools, because they are that; but, more specifically, they are divinatory tools, that is, tools that are used to answer questions.

With any of these tools, intuition, skill, and experience are needed. Astrology, numerology, palmistry, and to a lesser extent the Tarot require extensive study before they reveal their secrets. These tools require a teacher, whereas others, such as the *I Ching* and the Runes, can be learned on your own. Unless you are willing to undertake a serious study of astrology, numerology, palmistry, or the Tarot, it is best to rely on professionals for guidance from these tools and to stick to less complicated ones such as the *I Ching* and the Runes for getting guidance by yourself.

The reason for these guidelines is to impress you with the importance of getting adequate training with these tools. They are not toys. To use any of them like a toy is to invite trouble. And because it takes time to learn to use them properly, they are not something to dabble in. If you want to get information about your astrology chart, numbers, or palm, go to someone who has studied and practiced for years. Don't expect to be able to read your own chart, understand your numbers, analyze your own palm, or read Tarot cards by picking up a book and reading it.

This is a common mistake, which is responsible for misleading information—and for much misunderstanding about these tools. Some of the blame for this, however, lies with those who write books in this area. Many imply that you can learn how to read your chart, numbers, palm, or Tarot cards just by reading their book. However, as the saying goes, a little bit of knowledge can be a dangerous thing—or at the very least misleading. This is especially true with esoteric tools. Even extensive knowledge may not be enough; intuition and experience are needed as well. The highest use of these tools cannot be learned even by reading every book on the subject. Books, which by necessity rely heavily on a "cookbook" ("this means...") approach, only provide information; they cannot teach you how to synthesize that information. For this, intuition, experience, and a teacher are needed.

Using Divinatory Tools

The *I Ching* and the Runes are easier to learn to use than the other divinatory tool, the Tarot. All three can be learned on your own, but the *I Ching* and the Runes are the most alike and easiest to use. All divinatory tools allow you to ask questions of your Higher Self and receive a symbolic answer. With the *I Ching*, the answer comes in the form of a hexagram or hexagrams. With Runes, a glyph, or rune, which is engraved on a stone or piece of wood, provides the symbolic answer. And with the Tarot, the cards do.

Keeping a dated diary of your questions, results, and reflections will help you master these tools when starting out. As you become more comfortable with them, you still may benefit from keeping a record of your answers. Doing this is one way of affirming your seriousness and intent for help, which, as noted throughout this book, is crucial to receiving Spirit's guidance and healing.

For the same reason, establishing a ritual around your divination sessions is useful. You may want to light candles and incense, or sit on a special blanket or in front of an altar. Doing these things is a statement of reverence and receptivity. Of course, you also have to do them reverently, but these symbolic gestures draw out your reverence and affirm your faith in Spirit. And, of course, a prayer for guidance and an invocation for help is a good way to begin.

It is important to take plenty of time to formulate the question. The act of formulating a question is in itself enlightening, for in defining what you want to know, you learn something about yourself and your relationship to the object of inquiry. Always write the question down; this forces you to be very clear about what you are asking. Be specific in wording your question: As much as you can, specify who, what, when, where, and the time frame you are referring to.

When you ask a question of a divinatory tool, you can expect to receive understanding about your changing situation and your part in it. What is the best attitude or approach to take now about . . . ? What is this situation about for me now? and What do I need to be aware of now about . . . ? are the most appropriate kinds of questions. Notice that none of these expects an answer describing what will happen in the future. Questions can be asked about career, relationships, inner growth, finances, health, travel, social events, spiritual development, the life task, spiritual lessons, and other issues of concern—even political and worldly matters. However, avoid yes/no questions.

To get good results from any divinatory tool, proper mental preparation is necessary before posing the question and casting the coins, stones, or cards. The mind must be stilled and centered on the question for a while. How much time to take for this step depends on the person. For those used to

Tips for Studying Esoteric Systems

♦ Select one tool and concentrate on using only that tool. Each of these tools takes practice and time to develop. Focusing on one helps ensure that you will develop that one adequately.

♦ Get to know someone who is using that tool well. If you can, take classes from him or her. Use that person as a model for your approach to that tool. Good models may be hard to find, so keep looking until you find one. This is a very important step. It will determine your relationship to that tool.

♦ Get a quality bibliography from those in the field so that you can make the best of the time you spend learning. Information is spotty in this field; not every book you find will be helpful or even accurate. Shop as wisely for books as you do for a teacher.

♦ Read every good book on the subject that you can get your hands on.

♦ Study the charts, numbers, or palms of everyone you know. This will help you see what the personality traits and psychological issues you are reading about look like in real life. It will also help you remember what you are reading, because you will have living examples. Also, be sure to document your observations.

♦ Live with this tool. Make it part of your life. By living day in and day out for years with astrology or numerology, in particular, you learn about cycles and how the energies manifest over time. There is no substitute for experience.

♦ Don't expect to be able to use any esoteric tool to counsel others without having used it personally for at least five years. Of course, whether this is enough time depends on how absorbed you are in it during these five years. Even for a full-time student, this is not an unreasonable waiting period. No matter how serious a student you are, this much time is often needed just to get some perspective and experience with how the energies operate in the world. If you are not a serious student, I would suggest studying and living with it much longer than this.

♦ Get training in counseling if you are going to use this tool to counsel others. There is more to using these tools than having knowledge of the subject and a good intuition. Giving information to people is only so useful—and can even be harmful if it is not given with an appreciation of the person's psychological makeup and level of understanding.

becoming mentally still, a minute or two may be enough. Others less practiced in meditation may need several more minutes. Many prefer to use the yarrow stalk method of *I Ching* divination, for example, because it takes a half hour or more to perform, which allows plenty of time to meditate on the question. The purpose of becoming still is not so much to ensure that the coins, stones, or cards fall correctly as to increase receptivity to intuitions.

While casting the coins, stones, or cards, you should remain focused on your question and take plenty of time to gaze at the results; avoid jumping to conclusions or reacting from your intellect or emotions. While reading the appropriate text in the *I Ching* or *The Book of Runes*, or while gazing at the Tarot cards, note what words, phrases, or pictorial symbols stand out and become connected with an intuitive insight. Your intuitive insights usually will be coupled with a sense of rightness, of things "clicking," or a feeling of "aha!"

It's a good idea to jot down notes about the answer to help you remember it. Note taking can be helpful in clarifying the meaning you are getting intuitively. Continuing to rephrase these notes until they are just right is an excellent way to clarify intuitive insights.

Because of the ever-changing nature of life, the answer you receive will change if your attitude toward the situation changes significantly. Therefore, answers should only be taken in the context of the moment; they are not permanent or unalterable by any means. Just the act of asking a question may set in motion changes in attitudes and behavior that may change the outcome of the reading even moments later.

Also, be aware that about one chance in three produces a spread, a hexagram, or a rune that is not relevant to the question. This happens either because the person has not established a strong rapport with the tool or the tool is addressing another, more important, question. When this happens, it is often obvious. However, if you are not aware of this possibility, you may feel confused or upset by the irrelevant answer. You can begin again when this happens. However, because it is not good to establish a habit of asking the same question repeatedly, it is best to put these tools away for a while if you find yourself doing this. A good rule of thumb might be to put the tool away for the time being if a second try still produces confusing results.

R.L. Wing's *The I Ching Workbook* is my favorite book on the *I Ching*. It is not a direct translation of the *I Ching*, but its interpretations of the hexagrams are beautiful and easily understood. I highly recommend it if you choose to explore the *I Ching*. The Richard Wilhelm translation of the *I Ching* is favored by many and has a foreword by C.G. Jung; but it is difficult to understand, although it is beautifully poetic. The language in *The Book of Runes* is modern, positive, and easy to understand.

There are numerous Tarot decks. I suggest choosing one with positive images that do not have a fortunetelling focus. For purposes of interpretation, it is useful if the deck is fairly common; there are many obscure decks. The Rider-Waite deck is the most common.

Divinatory tools should be consulted with respect, and their answers allowed ample time to penetrate. They should never be used superficially or as a game, nor should they be consulted too often or the same question asked repeatedly.

To illustrate for you the kind of advice one might receive from the *I Ching*, I recently asked it this question: What do I need to know about my relationship with my publisher? I got out R.L. Wing's *The I Ching Workbook*, centered myself on the question, and tossed the coins six times. The tosses produced hexagram no. 61 "Chung Fu," or "Insight" (Inner Truth) in English, with no change lines. Here are the lines of the text that particularly spoke to me:

"The object here is to co-ordinate your forces so that there is a minimum of conflict and a maximum of effect."

"In yielding to the object of your inquiry, become totally open and unprejudiced toward its true nature."

"In relationships, base your camaraderie or friendship upon higher truths than simple interactions or idle pleasures. This will create firm and lasting bonds. Generally, it is an excellent time for establishing meaningful rapport with those around you and using energies thus exchanged for achieving significant deeds."

"Hence an open attitude achieves true penetration and insight into the situation."

Pitfalls in Using Divinatory Tools

The most common pitfall with divinatory tools is misreading them. This happens for many reasons, usually because of a lack of training, intuition, or objectivity. You need to be able to set aside your prejudices, feelings, desires, and thoughts about the issue in question, which is not always easy. This becomes easier when you practice meditation, which is another reason meditation is valuable.

Another problem is ascribing specific advice to the information you get. Even if you have correctly interpreted the symbols, you still may make unsound choices based on that interpretation or believe the divinatory tool has advised a specific course of action. This is never the case. Divinatory tools do not tell you what to do; they do not even tell you what not to do. They tell you what is manifesting at the moment you ask the question and what is likely to manifest at some point in the future if nothing else changes. They describe the situation you and others have created and point to likely ways of changing this if you don't like the outcome. This crucial distinction escapes many and is the cause for many of the problems with these tools.

Another pitfall is trying to use them to predict the future. Divinatory tools do not predict the future. This may sound ludicrous, since this is often how they have been used and what they have a reputation for doing. In fact, none of the esoteric tools can foretell the future, because the future can change at any moment if the choices of the people involved change. The future is in constant flux according to the free wills of those involved. Because of the many variables involved, trying to figure out what is going to happen in the future is a waste of time.

We can never know for certain what will happen, nor can we control it. Some of us will not be convinced of this though; the need to second-guess life is so great. This is the ego's need to control life to ensure safety and survival. It is an instinctive need in every human being, but one we are repeatedly shown cannot be met. We cannot ensure our future safety and security no matter what we do. Life is capable of infinite surprises. It brings us exactly what we need to learn, whether it is something we want or not.

Some people are convinced that the future can be foretold, because they know of times it has been. Their reasoning is that if the future can be known sometimes, then maybe it can be known anytime. But that doesn't follow. Only a few events in our lives are preordained, and the time and exact circumstances usually cannot be known much in advance, since they may be altered by the free will of those involved.

These preordained events may be described in Tarot cards, potentiated in astrological energies and numbers, encoded in palms, and read by psychics. The problem is that rarely is it helpful to know about them ahead of time. Knowing about them may actually interfere with the life plan, besides creating undue fear. Psychics, Tarot readers, astrologers, and others who tell people of such events often bear the responsibility of interfering with their plan—but that is part of their learning. So, yes, some events may be foretold. However, these events are generally not for us to know, particularly if they are painful.

Knowing about pleasant events is a slightly different matter. This knowledge can be encouraging and help us achieve our goals. One problem with this, though, is that this knowledge may change the outcome: If we are told we will succeed at something, we may not take the necessary steps to manifest that success, thinking it will just happen by itself.

An appropriate use of divinatory tools is to help us understand what purpose an event or circumstance is serving in our life. This is something our souls are trying to tell us intuitively, and something that will help us live more comfortably and effectively in the world. We may not always have the power to change circumstances or know about them in advance, but we do have the power to use those circumstances to grow and benefit ourselves and others.

On the other hand, sometimes we do have the power to change things. Events that are not preordained but likely to happen because our choices have already set them in motion are the things over which we have some control and which are beneficial to be aware of. The *I Ching*, the Runes, and the Tarot are helpful in describing what we are creating so that we can either continue creating it or make some changes. If we don't like what we are creating, we can make different choices and thereby reshape the future. These tools also can point to fruitful new directions.

Using these tools this way is empowering. Our power lies in accepting what we cannot change and in changing what we can, rather than trying to know what will happen. For many of us, this is a new way of approaching life. Instead of feeling victimized by life's unpredictable turns, we see that they have meaning for us. And we see that we are co-creating our life—if not determining every event, at least determining its effect on us. Life, then, becomes a mystery to be unraveled, a story in which we are both the player and the playwright. This frees up our energy from victimization and blame so that it can be used in our own transformation and in service to others.

Developing Your Intuition

We all are intuitive, but to varying degrees. Although esoteric tools can help us develop our intuition, no esoteric tool can make up for a lack of it. Esoteric tools are props for our intuition, ways to check or support it. Unless we already have a sense of our general direction, these tools may just confuse us. Fortunately, there are things we can do to develop our intuition. Developing our intuition is important, because it is one way our soul communicates to us. When our intuition is blocked, communication with our soul, or Higher Self, is blocked.

Intuition is developed by using it. However, this is not as simple as it sounds, since most people need to trust their intuition before they will use it (at least consciously). This is a double bind: If your first attempts at consciously using your intuition fail, you might conclude, "Never again!" and delay its development by not exercising it. Intuition is developed the same way many other abilities are: through trial and error. When we make an error, we have to pick ourselves (and our pride!) up, dust ourselves off, and try again. Developing intuition takes courage, patience, and time; but the rewards are worth it. Increasing your intuition will allow you to live a more fulfilling life and enable you to better help others too.

Developing Intuition

♥ Be willing to accept another way of knowing something besides intellectual knowing. Trust that this way of knowing is at least as valid as intellectual knowing. See your intuition as valuable and worth developing.

♥ Believe that you can develop it through your efforts. After all, if you don't believe you play any role in this, then you will not do anything to develop this skill—and it is a skill that is developed through effort and practice just like any other skill.

♥ Intend to develop it. Making an intention engages your will and opens you up to divine guidance and help in this matter. Intention and belief, as we have seen, are key in healing and in manifesting our desires.

♥ Make room for your intuition. Take time to be quiet and turn within: Take time to listen. This is such a simple principle but so important and easy to forget in our busy world.

(Cont'd next page)

♥ Learn to quiet your mind and emotions, and relax your body so that you can listen. Even if you make time and listen, if your channel is clogged with thoughts or disturbed by feelings, you will not be able to pick up intuitive messages. Learn to meditate!

♥ Be willing to receive messages even if they run contrary to what you want. Are you willing to receive guidance? Are you willing to make changes if necessary? Are you willing to be honest with yourself about what you receive?

♥ Maintain an attitude of non-attachment toward your intuitive impressions. Just receive, without judgment or attachment.

♥ Don't evaluate, judge, or interfere with your intuitive impressions as they arise.

♥ Learn to pay attention to your body and how it is reacting and responding subtly from moment to moment. Also, learn to be sensitive to the nuances of your feelings. Both our bodies and our feelings are capable of giving us intuitive messages. Notice your feelings and bodily reactions without trying to change them.

♥ Stay in the present and be aware of what is going on in the present moment.

♥ Become aware of your inner imagery. What pictures are being released into your conscious mind? Don't think about them or try to analyze them while they are emerging.

♥ Keep a journal of your intuitions. Whenever you receive an insight, write it down in your journal and review your journal regularly.

♥ Use visualization tapes, esoteric tools, and the creative arts to exercise and activate the right hemisphere of the brain, the part of the brain that relates to intuition. 3

Intuition is constantly at work in everyone to one degree or another. The more we can tap into this resource, the happier we will be and the smoother our lives will run. However, intuitions are sometimes unconsciously blocked or misinterpreted even in those whose intuition is well developed. Let's look at what creates these blocks.

Blocks to communication with our Higher Self are usually caused by negative emotions. However, on occasion, people lose track of their inner selves, because they have spun off on some "high" generated by positive feelings of infallibility, like the high of manic-depressives. These positive emotions can block access to the intuition as easily as negative emotions such as anger, depression, guilt, fear, and hatred. These highs are not generated by the soul, but by the ego as surely as negative emotions are. This phenomenon is worth noting, so that it is not confused with the happiness brought about by alignment with the soul.

Intuition is constantly at work in everyone to one degree or another. The more we can tap into this resource, the happier we will be and the smoother our lives will run. However, intuitions are sometimes unconsciously blocked or misinterpreted even in those whose intuition is well developed. Let's look at what creates these blocks.

Blocks to communication with our Higher Self are usually caused by negative emotions. However, on occasion, people lose track of their inner selves, because they have spun off on some "high" generated by positive feelings of infallibility, like the high of manic-depressives. These positive emotions can block access to the intuition as easily as negative emotions such as anger, depression, guilt, fear, and hatred. These highs are not generated by the soul, but by the ego as surely as negative emotions are. This phenomenon is worth noting, so that it is not confused with the happiness brought about by alignment with the soul.

The way we know we are aligned with our soul is by how we feel, although our feelings, as just noted, still need to be examined. Feelings of happiness, joy, peace, contentment, and excitement are indications of alignment. Contrarily, depression and anger may be due to being out of alignment with our soul's plan. Depression and anger also may be due to our ego not getting its way, to negative thinking, or to unresolved feelings and experiences from our past.

Whenever you have a feeling, examine it for its source. Why do you feel this way now? What is behind it? What does it say about what you need to do? If you have created it by negative thinking or if you are throwing a tantrum because you aren't getting your way in the world, these questions will reveal that. If something else is behind it, something that harkens back to a deep spiritual need, then something in your life needs to change if you are to be happy. If you make that change and feel happy about it, then you know you did the right thing. If you still are unhappy, then you need to ask more questions.

This is primarily an intuitive process, which is why you can easily be mistaken. But if you hold back and don't risk following what you believe will make you truly happy, you probably won't learn the truth. Sometimes the only way to find out what we need for true happiness is to risk going after the wrong thing. Doing this eventually teaches us how our intuition works. Still, some healing of emotional issues may be necessary before this process works as smoothly as it can.

We all have emotional wounds, originating either in this life or others—usually both. These wounds generate negative thoughts and feelings, which interfere with our connection—and communication—with Spirit. These wounds are reflected in the aura as energy blockages, which constrict the flow of energy in the aura. They arise from:

♦ Unhealed emotional trauma in past lives and the present one,

♦ Negative thought patterns, also often instigated by trauma in the past, and

♦ Negative feelings accumulated over a long period of time, often resulting in long-standing negative thought patterns.

Even if past-life issues have already been healed, everyone in this society has emotional wounds that need healing, because we live in a sick society. No one goes unscathed. We all are touched by the neuroses of our culture, which show up as guilt, self-hatred, addictions, escapism, and destructive and violent impulses. So, we all have healing to do if we are to live free and happy lives, and, particularly, if we are to fulfill our life purpose. Because our wounds distort and disturb the functioning of our intuition, they need to be healed if we are to find fulfillment.

The severity of these auric blockages varies, depending on how long they have been present, what caused them, and whether they are being reinforced. If they are severe enough, they can cause actual physical illness, not just emotional congestion and negativity.

These blocks interfere with intuition by creating negative feedback that travels through the unconscious mind to the conscious mind and appears as fears, guilt, negative thoughts, self-hatred, and other negative emotions. If they are severe, the mind becomes assaulted with negativity, which inhibits or muddies other communication from the unconscious. It's like having your soul's channel of communication clogged with negativity. And as all meditators know, when the mind is full of anything, Spirit cannot be heard or experienced. The trouble is not only that the mind is busy, however, but what it is busy with. Negative thoughts are not merely annoying, but often lead to negative or counterproductive actions. Negative thoughts, when we believe them, often determine when and where we will put our energy and how effective we will be.

So, the first step in making our intuition more accessible is getting emotionally healthy. This means clearing past traumas, reprogramming negative thoughts and conditioning, and becoming aware of our psychological needs. All these take time (sometimes lifetimes) and development, which is why our intuition generally improves as we evolve and become more aware.

The intellect also interferes with receiving intuitive messages. The intellect becomes engaged immediately after an intuition is discharged from the unconscious mind to the conscious mind. As soon as the intuition enters the realm of the conscious mind, it is translated into familiar symbols—usually words, pictures, or feelings. The words given to intuitive impressions may be inaccurate, as may the words given to any pictures or feelings that arise. Thus, although pictures and feelings are a rather pure form of communication from the unconscious, they might not be translated properly into language. Sometimes they are not translated properly because of unresolved emotional issues. In other cases, they are misinterpreted, because the ego has a need to hear something. The need may be a culturally conditioned one, one stemming from astrological energies, or the need to please someone.

There are already many good books on the market with specific exercises for developing your intuition and psychic abilities (see bibliography), so I will not offer any specific ones here. However, be aware that actively developing your intuition and psychic abilities can be a stormy process. You may be led down many blind alleys, and you also may lead others down blind alleys if you are not careful. You are bound to come face to face with an important lesson: correct use of power.

Abuse of power and other pitfalls of intuitive development can be avoided by examining your motives for wanting to develop your intuition or psychic abilities and by asking for the qualities you want to develop, such as humility and devotion to God. Aligning yourself daily with your soul through meditation will ensure that you use your intuitive abilities for the good of all, especially if you ask for this in your meditation. Meditating on God—on goodness—aligns us with good and creates a longing for God, which counteracts the ego's cravings. Not doing this while developing your psychic abilities is dangerous. People who fail to align themselves with God can cause great harm and fall very hard. Your soul will let you learn this the hard way if you choose.

CHAPTER 6 NOTES

1. Tracy Marks, *Planetary Aspects: From Conflict to Cooperation* (Sebastopol, Calif.: CRCS Publications, 1987), p. 185.

2. Barbara Schermer, *Astrology Alive: Experiential Astrology, Astrodrama, and the Healing Arts* (England: The Aquarian Press, 1989), p. 55.

3. Frances E. Vaughan, *Awakening Intuition*, (Garden City, N.Y.: Doubleday & Co., 1979), p. 203-205.

CHAPTER 6 SOURCES

Marks, Tracy. *Planetary Aspects: From Conflict to Cooperation.* Sebastopol, Calif.: CRCS Publications, 1987.

Schermer, Barbara. *Astrology Alive! Experiential Astrology, Astro-drama and the Healing Arts.* England: The Aquarian Press, 1988.

Vaughan, Frances E. *Awakening Intuition.* Garden City, N.Y.: Doubleday & Co., 1979.

Wing, R.L. *The I Ching Workbook.* Garden City, N.Y.: Doubleday & Co., 1979.

CHAPTER 6 SUGGESTED READING

The Tarot

Guiley, Rosemary Ellen. *The Mystical Tarot.* New York: Penguin Books, 1991.

Lawrence, D. Baloti. *Tarot: 22 Steps to a Higher Path.* Stamford, Conn.: Longmeadow Press, 1992.

Nichols, Sallie. *Jung and Tarot: An Archetypal Journey.* York Beach, Maine: Samuel Weiser, 1980.

Pollack, Rachel. *Seventy-Eight Keys of Wisdom: A Book of Tarot.* London: The Aquarian Press, 1980.

Riley, Jana. *The Tarot Book: Basic Instruction for Reading Cards.* York Beach, Maine: Samuel Weiser, 1992.

Palmistry

Hipskind, Judith. *Palmistry: The Whole View.* St. Paul: Llewellyn,

1988.

Hoffman, Enid. *Hands: A Complete Guide to Palmistry.* West Chester, Penn.: Whitford Press, 1983.

Reid, Lori. *The Complete Book of the Hand: A Modern Approach to Hand Analysis.* London: Pan Books, 1991.

Reid, Lori. *How to Read Hands.* London: Aquarian Press, 1985.

Numerology

Javane, Faith and Dusty Bunker. *Numerology and the Divine Triangle.* West Chester, Penn.: Whitford Press, 1979.

Jordan, Juno. *Numerology: The Romance in Your Name.* Marina del Rey, Calif.: De Vorss & Co., 1989.

Roquemore, Kathleen. *It's All in Your Numbers: The Secrets of Numerology.* New York: Harper & Row, 1985.

The I Ching

Blofeld, John, ed. and trans. *I Ching: The Book of Change.* New York: E.P. Dutton & Co., 1968.

Reifler, Sam. *I Ching: A New Interpretation for Modern Times.* New York: Bantam Books, 1985.

Wilhelm, Richard. *The I Ching,* trans. Cary F. Baynes. Princeton, N.J.: Princeton University Press, 1981.

Wing, R.L. *The I Ching Workbook.* Garden City, N.Y.: Doubleday & Co., 1979.

The Runes

Blum, Ralph. *The Book of Runes: A Handbook for the Use of an Ancient Oracle.* New York: St. Martin's, 1987.

Intuition

Carrington, Hereward. *Your Psychic Powers and How to Develop Them*. Brooklyn: Templestar Co., 1958.

Hoffman, Enid. *Expand Your Psychic Skills*. West Chester, Penn.: Whitford Press, 1987.

Vaughan, Frances E. *Awakening Intuition*. Garden City, N.Y.: Anchor Press, 1979.

Astrology

Arroyo, Stephen. *Astrology, Karma, and Transformation: The Inner Dimensions of the Birth Chart*. Sebastopol, Calif.: CRCS Publications, 1978.

Arroyo, Stephen. *Astrology, Psychology & the Four Elements: An Energy Approach to Astrology and Its Use in the Counseling Arts*. Sebastopol, Calif.: CRCS Publications, 1975.

Hickey, Isabel M. *Astrology, a Cosmic Science*. Sebastopol, Calif.: CRCS Publications, 1992.

Oken, Alan. *Alan Oken's Complete Astrology*. New York: Bantam Books, 1988.

Marks, Tracy. *The Astrology of Self-Discovery*. Sebastopol, Calif.: CRCS Publications, 1985.

Marks, Tracy. *Planetary Aspects: From Conflict to Cooperation*. Sebastopol, Calif.: CRCS Publications, 1987.

Pottenger, Maritha. *Astro Essentials: Planets in Signs, Houses and Aspects*. San Diego: ACS Publications, 1991.

Sasportas, Howard. *The Gods of Change: Pain, Crisis, and the Transits of Uranus, Neptune and Pluto*. London: Arkana Books, 1989.

Starck, Marcia. *Astrology: Key to Holistic Health*. Birmington, Michigan: Seek-It, 1982.

CHAPTER 7
Aligning with Your Soul's Plan

Aligning with our soul's plan is critical to healing—and to happiness. We have explored how astrology, esoteric tools, guided visualization, and shamanic journeying can help us with this. In this chapter, we will examine how channels and psychics also can help. But first we will look at how our soul communicates to us and then explore what is involved in the soul's plan.

How Spirit Communicates

Much of our pain would be alleviated if we could communicate with our soul. If we knew the purpose behind our experiences (or even if we knew for certain there was one), we could live more comfortably in the world. Making peace with life depends on being able to see beyond outward appearances to the underlying meaning. Contrary to what it may seem sometimes, we are not left alone with our struggles. Spirit is ever-present, moving through our experiences, and guiding us in learning from them and in reaching our goals. Not recognizing Spirit's presence is what creates pain, in addition to misconstruing the meaning behind events. So much pain is created and time wasted by misinterpreting events—time which could be spent in joyous appreciation of life rather than lamentation. How much simpler life would be if we understood our experiences! But we are here to learn how to do this. This is one of life's lessons.

The soul is always trying to communicate understanding to us. Our task is to learn to listen. We do this by listening with our heart. This kind of listening is not so different from listening with our ears. Stillness and receptivity are necessary, as with ordinary listening. After all, you cannot hear if your ears, mouth, or mind are already occupied. Inner listening is the same way. You must close off sensory and mental stimulation to hear what your heart has to say.

"Listening with your heart" is more than a pretty metaphor. There is an etheric center in the heart region, aptly called the heart center, which some say is the seat of the soul within the human body. Intuitive messages from the soul are registered in this center. By turning your attention to this spot in your body, you can learn to interpret these messages.

For most people, intuitive messages don't come in the form

of words; however, they are not far from words, since the mind translates them almost immediately into words—or thoughts. Although mistakes are sometimes made during translation, with practice everyone learns to translate intuitive messages. Eventually, you learn that if the feeling in your heart center doesn't match your interpretation, you are off track. Then you have to go back, pose the question again, and listen again.

It is no mystery that answers to questions can be received intuitively. People have always been able to communicate with their Higher Self, or soul. There have been times in history, however, when people were unaware of this and relied on others for answers. This is not true today. More people than ever are capable of receiving messages for themselves and others, and more are willing to be guided by them. This is a hopeful sign, as these times call for alignment with our spiritual selves, too long lost.

Communication Through Dreams

Dreams are another way our souls communicate with us. The unconscious mind, where dreams are formed, is a bridge between the superconscious mind (the realm of the Higher Self) and the conscious mind. Messages from our Higher Self travel from the superconscious mind to the unconscious mind, where they take the form of symbols, feelings, or other impressions. During sleep, with the help of spirit guides, the Higher Self's messages are translated into visual symbols and incorporated into dreams.

So, imbedded in the symbolism of some of your dreams are messages to you from your soul, or your Higher Self. These messages may not be obvious to you, but that rarely matters. Although working with your dreams is helpful, even if you don't, your dreams affect your unconscious mind. Your unconscious mind understands these messages, which have the power to steer you in a certain direction without you even being aware of them. So, some dreams are used to guide us, whether or not we remember or understand them.

Nevertheless, it is still valuable to acknowledge and record our dreams. By recording our dreams, we assist the communication between the superconscious and conscious minds. And we are affirming: Yes, I believe Spirit is working through my dreams, and I want to know what Spirit is saying to me. Even if you don't write down your dreams, this affirmation is valuable. However, making the effort to observe and understand your dreams, reinforces this affirmation.

Our dreams have much to teach us. They not only bring us messages from our Higher Self, but they help us process the day's events as well as mirror an exaggerated version of our personal self. Our dreams present us with a caricature of ourselves, portraying our personal, psychological issues. In pointing out our issues, dreams provide us with useful information for our growth.

Communication Through Other People

Spirit also communicates with us through other people. This may sound odd, but just as we receive intuitions consciously or unconsciously, so do others, who pass them on to us often unknowingly. People are remarkably receptive to intuitions, especially when the information doesn't apply directly to them. Information about yourself is often received more clearly by others than by you. This is why consulting with others when you feel confused is helpful.

So, other people, regardless of their development, often become mouthpieces for Spirit. When they are acting in this capacity, there will be a sense of inner resonance and rightness about what they are saying, like someone just turned on a light. There also may be feelings of relaxation, peace, excitement, and joy. These feelings are signs that truth has been spoken. They are the same feelings that arise when your intuition is working properly.

A less direct method Spirit delivers messages through others to us is by inspiring them to do something that sparks something in us. For instance, we have all had books come to us at just the right time. Or maybe we have heard about the perfect job just "by accident." Many of the circumstances in our daily life are created by others who have been inspired intuitively to create them. This is one way the soul guides each of us along our path.

Communication Through Symbols

Spirit also communicates to us through symbols, similar to the symbols in our dreams. These symbols come to us through art, music, and everyday life. How often have you been stirred into remembering something you had forgotten just as your eyes fell on some object? Spirit is capable of guiding our eyes and timing our actions in a way that makes use of objects in our environment to deliver messages. And how often have the words of a song had a special importance to you at a particular moment? Spirit is capable of alerting us to certain things in our environment by working through our unconscious.

Although we sometimes misinterpret these signs or assign meaning when none exists, it is important that we stay open to messages from our Higher Self. The more we acknowledge Spirit's presence in our life, the more we will be able to benefit from signs like these. These signs or symbols, like the symbols in our dreams, affect us unconsciously and inspire us to do things without understanding why we are doing them. Because symbols affect the unconscious rather than the conscious mind, it may be hard to appreciate their impact. But that doesn't mean they don't have one.

In fact, symbols, which bypass the conscious mind, are more likely to have the intended effect than more direct means of communication, because they don't meet with conscious resistance. Sometimes when we are aware of what Spirit is saying to us, we discount it, ignore it, or resist it. This doesn't happen when the meaning of a symbol is received by the unconscious. Because of this, whether you intend to work in cooperation with Spirit or not, you invariably do. This explains why most people follow their soul's plan even when they have little awareness of it or even of its existence.

Communication Through Feelings

One of the most important ways Spirit communicates with us is through our feelings, which is why emotional healing is so important to spiritual growth and to fulfillment. Our soul guides us with both pleasant and painful feelings. When we choose a direction contrary to our soul's plan, we may experience emotional discomfort, such as sadness, disappointment, depression, or grief. These are feelings we should pay attention to—

particularly grief. A sense of grief is nearly always present when we have taken a wrong turn and persist in that direction. These feelings may be out of proportion to any loss we may be experiencing or seem to come from nowhere, from no apparent loss. Feelings of grief that are out of proportion or have no real connection to events in our life may mean our soul is trying to tell us something. Unlike normal feelings of grief, these don't go through the usual stages and eventually subside, but linger and often increase if we persist in the same choices.

Since the soul's plan is broad, falling so far off track to warrant such a signal is uncommon. Deep, long-lasting feelings of grief are usually a last-ditch effort on the part of the soul to communicate its needs, needs that probably have been long ignored. This kind of grieving is especially important to do something about, since it signals a significant departure from what will make us happy and fulfilled. Because of this, nothing is likely to quell it except appropriate changes, although many try to dull it with drugs or alcohol. This is one cause of substance abuse and why it is rightly called a spiritual disease. What is sad is that drugs and alcohol only make matters worse by further alienating people from their feelings.

Feelings like joy, elation, and excitement confirm our alignment with our soul's plan. They also won't necessarily be in proportion to or related to obvious conditions in our life. They arise whenever we do something that establishes us more firmly on our path. This path is wide, with not nearly as many wrong choices as we might imagine and many more right ones than we probably realize. Whenever we find one of these ways, our soul sends us feelings of elation as encouragement to continue and as confirmation of our spiritual needs. We can change this course anytime and still feel good if the new direction continues to fulfill our spiritual needs.

As long as we get the messages our soul is sending through our feelings, intuition, dreams, and other means, the soul won't have to find other ways to communicate. But if we don't, the soul may take a more drastic approach. It may create circumstances that awaken us to looking at our life anew. These circumstances may be mildly unpleasant or of crisis proportions, depending on what is needed. Obviously, no one wants to be shocked into finding his or her life path, but sometimes this is necessary.

Some of the more common, less severe, incentives we receive to reevaluate our lives are disgruntled spouses, financial strains, bosses becoming impossible to work for, or friends or family moving. More drastic catalysts are physical injuries, brushes with death, terminal illnesses, losing a loved one through death or divorce, losing physical functioning, being unable to continue our occupation, or significant financial loss or destruction of our property.

With any of the more severe catalysts, our life is changed forever. We can never go back to the way it was, as much as we might try. We have to build anew, create new structures, and reformulate our thinking. Often a period of healing is needed before the rebuilding can begin, which entails letting go of the old and reordering our life. Priorities shift, new ideas emerge, and eventually a new plan is born. The grieving process gives birth to a new life, one that will have room for the new direction that is trying to emerge.

During the grieving process, people gradually let go of their old ideas about themselves and their lives and eventually reach out with hope for a new direction. The time it takes to reach this point varies from person to person. Some cling desperately to the old rather than look ahead, certain that the future holds nothing for them. Fortunately, the soul has ways of introducing new possibilities and excitement into the lives of even those who are most rigid and fearful.

Crises give birth to new possibilities. The soul uses pivotal times like these to present opportunities potentially rich in fulfillment and happiness. It is worthwhile for those going through any crisis to pay attention to the kinds of opportunities that arise; they may be clues to the new direction trying to emerge. Paying particular attention to coincidences and themes can lead you out of the confusion of these times. Anything your soul is trying to tell you will be repeated several ways, perhaps by a number of different people, perhaps by a number of different coincidences.

During times of transition and crisis, the soul uses every method available to reach you with new ideas and help you establish a new direction in your life if that is the purpose of your crisis. Most people are more receptive to suggestions during these times, because they see they cannot go back to their old lives. Some, on the other hand, remain closed, fearful, and victimized. This stance is clearly a choice, one everyone has the right to make, but a painful one. Eventually, most let go of it.

What usually keeps someone from letting go of this stance is a heavily fortressed denial system. When the fear of one's denial system breaking down is greater than any other fear or more important than fulfillment, the soul stands little chance of making headway toward a new beginning. In these instances, although the person cannot go back to life as it was, he or she will pretend to—and pretend to be happy. Unless people are honest about their feelings, the soul cannot influence them through their feelings. Denial is a formidable opponent of growth.

Soul communication depends on people being honest with themselves about their feelings. Not doing this is the most common reason people lose their direction. And once they are off the path, they create reasons to remain there: They claim (and pretend) to be happy, they believe they cannot survive under any other arrangement, and they profess attachments to their way of life. But they will never have true happiness if they are not fulfilling their spiritual plan. That is the saddest thing of all.

Many people settle for much less than they have to. Many don't reach high enough: They don't believe life can be better; they don't believe that happiness is for them. Ironically, or maybe not so ironically, living one or more lifetimes like this creates a drive for fulfillment and determination to get more out of life. So eventually, people who make this choice learn by the consequences to choose differently in another lifetime. But why wait until then! Life is for living. Why not trust your feelings, your spirit? Why not trust that happiness can be yours? Everyone can live a fulfilled life.

The Soul's Plan

Everyone has a destiny. This doesn't mean living out some predestined story conceived before life, however. Although our destiny is conceived before life, it is done so only in broad brush strokes. Creating the details of it is the adventure called life. With the freedom we have to flesh out our destiny, we also have the freedom to ignore it or to follow some other course.

So, to say that you have chosen a certain destiny before life neither implies that it will be fulfilled nor that it is known how it will be fulfilled. It is all up to you.

It is hard to ignore our destiny. It continually calls to us, and unseen forces drop messages about it here and there. Sometimes we notice these clues and sometimes we don't. When we miss them, we lose out on valuable opportunities for growth and fulfillment. The advantage of knowing our soul's direction is that we can use the opportunities and resources it makes available to us to unfold it: We can work in cooperation with it, which is the easiest way. By being open to it and by fanning our desire to work in accordance with it, we can greatly increase our chances of accomplishing it as well as our happiness, ease, and fulfillment.

What I am calling destiny is your soul's plan, a set of goals and lessons you chose before life. The soul's plan is general; the specifics are not known before life but are determined by the choices you make every day. Thus, our lives are created by an interweaving of the soul's plan and free will.

The Life Task

The life task is one special goal chosen as part of the soul's plan that, if accomplished, will advance our spiritual evolution. There are, of course, many ways each of us can advance our evolution and therefore many possible life tasks.

To help you identify your life task, it will be useful to know what kinds of life tasks exist. There are three categories of life tasks: lessons, talents, and service, with subdivisions under each (see following page).

3 Kinds of Life Tasks

1 LESSONS

Learning the basic lessons of human evolution.

Correcting negative behavior patterns or beliefs from previous lifetimes.

Balancing karma.

2 TALENTS

Developing talents or special abilities.

Developing qualities, virtues, or attributes.

3 SERVICE

Developing the right attitude toward service.

Serving others and society with our talents.

Lessons

The basic lessons of human evolution are described by the twelve signs. Rather than just listing the lessons of human evolution, the following chart organizes these lessons under the signs of the zodiac. Learning any of these lessons may be someone's life task.

Lessons According to Sign

Aries is learning self-sufficiency, independence, leadership, and initiative; and developing physical strength and prowess.

Taurus is learning to provide for one's material needs and comforts, and develop values.

Gemini is learning to think, communicate, and teach.

Cancer is developing compassion and the ability to bond with others, learning about feelings, and learning how to care for others and be cared for.

Leo is learning to create, organize, express oneself, and lead.

Virgo is learning humility and service, practical skills and craftsmanship, and care of one's health.

Libra is learning about personal love and cooperation, developing kindness, and learning aesthetic appreciation and social graces.

Scorpio is learning to be intimate, to trust, to share, and to use power and the will correctly.

Sagittarius is learning about the world, philosophy, religion, and law; and learning to share wisdom and understanding with others.

Capricorn is learning to make one's way in the world, and to be hard-working, responsible, patient, practical, cautious, realistic, and persevering.

Aquarius is learning to work in groups, and manifest one's ideals and ideas in the world.

Pisces is learning compassion, psychic sensitivity, humanitarian service, and love for God.

I will leave you to distill the many possible life tasks from this list. You can see that the twelve signs not only represent the basic lessons of human evolution, but also the many talents. So, Aries, for example, is not only about learning selfhood but also about developing the talent to forge ahead fearlessly into new areas. Each sign also represents a particular path of service. Aries, for instance, true to its pioneering spirit, might serve by leading in the fight for freedom or for a cure for AIDS.

Talents

To help you envision other possible life tasks, a list of talents as they relate to the signs appears on the facing page. Each of these talents takes lifetimes to develop. Once someone has developed a talent, it is likely to be used in a life task that serves humanity. The purpose of developing talents is ultimately to serve.

As you can imagine, there are almost as many life tasks as there are individuals, but the most common ones are contained in these lists of lessons and talents. You will want to know more than just your sun sign, however, which is the only thing most people know about their charts. You will also want to know the themes of your chart, which include your moon sign and rising sign (which also is called the Ascendant), among other possible themes.

Blocks to Fulfilling Your Destiny

Sometimes our beliefs or ideas about life prevent us from fulfilling our life task. One of these is the belief that you can't trust yourself to know what is best for you—and that might even be true, at least at first. Many people don't know what is best for them until they begin to experiment with what they think they want. There is no better way to discover what you want than to go after what you think you want—you will soon find out whether that desire was appropriate. Everyone must learn to discriminate between the soul's desires and the ego's desires as well as his or her conditioning. The only way to do this is to practice. So, expect to make some mistakes; that is how we learn.

Don't let anything stand in the way of following what you

Talents According to Sign

Aries: physical strength, athletic prowess, leadership, a fighting spirit, and the power to give birth to projects and ideas.

Taurus: business acumen, common sense, the power to bring ideas into physical form and carry out plans, endurance, aesthetic appreciation, and artistic talent.

Gemini: intellectual and verbal aptitude, a flair for writing and teaching, wit, knowledge, and adaptability.

Cancer: compassion, psychic sensitivity, kindness, sympathy, and an ability to nurture others.

Leo: creativity, artistic talents, leadership, courage, organizational and managerial ability, and a talent for entertainment.

Virgo: humility, simplicity, efficiency, thoroughness, craftsmanship, dedication, orderliness, selfless service, and an understanding of health and healing.

Libra: artistic talents, an aesthetic sense, a sweet and harmonious nature, an ability to see all sides, a love of justice, and a talent for counseling and mediation.

Scorpio: psychological and metaphysical understanding, psychic powers and sensitivity, self-mastery, healing power, and financial acumen.

Sagittarius: sagacity, writing and teaching ability, philosophical and metaphysical understanding, oratory skills, and a keen intellect.

Capricorn: business and financial acumen, organizational and leadership ability, and a flair for politics.

Aquarius: a passion for social reform, an ability to work with all kinds of people, and the power to invent and bring forth ideas that improve society.

Pisces: compassion, psychic sensitivity, selfless service, spiritual understanding, and a deep love for God.

believe is your soul's desire. If you find out you were wrong, then you will be that much closer to knowing what your true desire is. We all have to learn to trust ourselves if we are ever to feel the satisfaction of unfolding our destiny. So, don't let not trusting yourself stand in the way of taking steps toward your goal. You won't get there without taking some risks!

Another belief that can keep us from recognizing our destiny is the belief that only a few, select people have a meaningful destiny, while the rest of us are doomed to ordinary lives. In truth, fulfillment comes in doing whatever our life task is. Often it is something ordinary and commonplace such as parenting or learning to be more intimate with our partner. It may even be a number of different things at different periods in our life. In any event, everyone has a destiny that is personally meaningful. So, you are not doomed to unhappiness if you don't have a glamorous life task. But, you may be doomed to unhappiness if you don't surrender to your life task, whatever it may be. When you do, you will be granted the happiness and peace you long for.

The beauty of life is that we each can be happy. But we each will find happiness in our own way: What makes one person happy will not necessarily make another happy. What is important is that we each pursue our own personal happiness—whatever that may be. We will then be assured of fulfilling our life task. The hardest part of life may be getting up the courage to do what makes us happy!

To find this happiness, and consequently our life task, we also may need to drop the habit of living in a world of ideas—many of them unrealistic—of what we think our life or life in general should be like. These mental creations are based largely on what parents and society (via television and the media) tell us about what we should be like and what we should want. But reality will never match most of these mental creations. As long as we hold them as prerequisites for happiness, we will never be happy. We will be so preoccupied with trying to live up to these images that we will miss living the life we were meant to live.

A good example of this is the image of the perfectly formed, well endowed, svelte female with abundant tresses that many women hold in their mind and aspire to but can never live up to. Advertising, in particular, has conditioned women to believe that they must look a certain way to be beautiful—and lovable.

Although visualizing something we want to create can help us achieve it, holding an unattainable image in mind is not an affirmation of anything, except maybe of our inadequacies. These unrealistic ideas and images need to be eliminated from our thinking.

Affirmations can help counteract unrealistic and unsuitable ideas like this one, which take energy away from achieving our true goals and prevent us from knowing our true desires. An affirmation like "God made me in His/Her perfect image of beauty for me" could be used to counteract the idea that we should fit someone else's image of beauty. This frees our energy for more relevant, life-enhancing matters.

Something else that can interfere with discovering and unfolding our life task is a lack of will, or passivity. Often behind passivity is the credo: If I don't commit, I won't fail. This is one of the more insidious beliefs, since it is usually unconscious. The result is someone who dabbles in this and that but never gets fully involved in anything. In pretending they are already fulfilled, these people may fool others, but they cannot fool themselves. Facing the truth can be the hardest and most important thing they ever do. If this describes you, affirmations can help you get beyond this block. You can word the affirmation any way you like, as long as it affirms your belief in a life task and your commitment to unfolding it. It is that simple, but quite a hurdle for some.

When you examine your actions, you will find that they are driven primarily by feelings and intuitions. You may think that thoughts drive your actions, but behind most thoughts are feelings and intuitions. These are what steer you, what drive you, what shape your life. And these come from your soul. Once you attune to this force that drives you, it is impossible to deny its existence or power. It is the force behind all life and the force that connects all of us in this intricate web we call life. It is love.

Love is what moves us, lights our path, whispers in our ear. Love is the force that moves all creation toward its chosen destiny and toward a common evolution and plan. Love is behind it all. Call it God, call it Spirit, call it destiny, call it anything you will. The name doesn't change what it is, nor that it is knowable in each of us.

This force can be felt within us. Feeling it is our joy; blocking it is our death. We are never more alive than when we feel this eternal and all pervasive force in us and about us. The goal of our evolution is to become aware of it and merge with it. Living with it, flowing with it, is all we need to be happy. We don't need acclaim or money or even friends if we are expressing it and moving with it. Happily, however, these also are often part of living in tune with our spiritual nature, as spiritual fulfillment brings with it all manner of happiness.

If we follow our feelings of joy, expansion, love, and goodness, we cannot go wrong. Inside each of us is such a force for good that if we allow ourselves to feel it, we would know the world is in good hands. Tap into this force in meditation and see.

The good inside us is calling us to be who we came here to be, to be this and to be this to the best of our ability. When we do follow our heart's desire, we will discover an undreamed of courage and strength. This is our soul's support, the gift of being aligned with our path. This is what bolsters us in times of trouble. We can draw on this strength to face the other challenges in our life. Being aligned with our path makes all other difficulties easier to face.

One other reason for you to find your life task and do it is that others are waiting for you to play your role, so that they can play theirs. We are not alone on our path. Others are traveling with us and they need us to play our part. If we don't, others may or may not take over for us. But even if others do take over for us, it wouldn't be the same. We are meant for our plan and our plan is meant for us. So, let us claim our place in it.

We are not replaceable in this plan. Nothing in the web is replaceable or unimportant. Whatever we choose to do with our life will be noticed by the rest of creation and affected by it. We not only have a responsibility to ourselves to find and fulfill our plan, but also to everyone and everything in this magnificent web.

Channels and Psychics

Sometimes we need additional help understanding our plan and our experiences. Channels or psychics can be helpful, but you have to be careful about who you go to. Like astrologers and others in this field, channels and psychics do not have to be credentialed or certified. No one is there to tell them whether or not they are ready to counsel people. No one but the consumer is there to evaluate their psychic gifts either, which can be anywhere from fraudulent to remarkable. Some guidelines to help you choose a channel or psychic are given in the last chapter.

A good channel or psychic can be an important resource in understanding your experiences and life plan. However, not every channel, psychic, or other esoteric counselor is able to get this kind of information for you. Many people who call themselves psychics only tell you what you are creating. They don't give you guidance about your soul's plan or point out your role in what you are creating. Few ever suggest you can reshape it by your choices. Many use fatalistic language, which reinforces people's fears and feelings of powerlessness. Psychic readers also often give out information about set events that should not be revealed. This happens because many psychics lack spiritual understanding or don't have an adequate esoteric background.

Many psychics have been born with gifts but have had no training in using them. Therefore, not all psychics will be knowledgeable about using their gifts to help people understand their life plans. This, coupled with the fact that many psychics are just plain inaccurate, makes going to people who call themselves psychics risky and sometimes harrowing.

Channels may have a different problem getting this kind of information. They may not be in contact with an entity who is capable of giving this kind of guidance, but who will try anyway. There are many competent channels who are channeling lesser developed guides who are not very skilled at advising humans. Some channels are even involved with lower astral entities, people who have crossed over and are awaiting rebirth, who are even less likely to be helpful. Would you want advice from just anyone who has crossed over?

Those who are able to help you with your questions concerning your life plan and your growth are entities on the higher astral plane and beyond who have had sufficient experience acting as guides for humans. However, you, as a consumer, cannot know for sure who the channel is contacting, even if he or she tells you, because sometimes the channel is deceived or is unable to reach a high level of intelligence due to fatigue, illness, or carelessness.

Besides carefully selecting a channel, by getting referrals and interviewing the channel before making an appointment, there are several things you can do to ensure that you have a positive and beneficial session.

Preparing for a Session with a Channel

♦ Come to the session prepared with questions. Think over carefully what you want to ask, why you want to ask it, and how you will ask it. Your questions will determine the kind of information you will receive. Most channeled entities insist on questions, because they will not give you information you have not requested. Giving unsolicited information is considered an infringement on free will. So, be wary of any channeled entity who is determined to tell you about things that you have not asked about or given your permission to speak about.

♦ Don't expect to receive specific information about other people. If it serves your growth, you may receive some information about someone else. However, if your motives for asking are not pure, you will receive nothing at all. It would be too much like invading someone's privacy, and high level beings will not do that.

♦ Don't expect to receive specifics about the future either. General trends with vague references about timing can be received. However, even this information is subject to change as variables change. Specific personal information about the future should call into question the credibility of the channel or the channel's source, since high level beings do not indulge in telling people specifically what is going to happen to them.

♦ You may not get accurate past-life information. Past-life information is difficult even for higher astral beings to read. High level beings sometimes give very specific information

(Cont'd. next page)

about past lives if it serves the person's growth. Even so, the information could be mistaken. Low level beings will give you any information you ask for, but it won't necessarily be correct. If past-life information resonates strongly within you, then it is likely to be correct or at least useful to you. If not, then don't accept it.

♦ Don't expect specific advice about what to do. High level beings will not tell you what to do. If you are told anything in a way that precludes your free choice or chooses for you, this is reason to question the channel or the channel's source. The best way to avoid this is not to ask about specific choices you are considering. (i.e. Should I move to L.A. or San Francisco?) It is tempting to ask others what to do, especially if you assume they know what you should do better than you. However, making our own choices is an important part of our evolution. This is something that will be acknowledged by any high level being. Getting information about your growth and needs so that you can choose more wisely should be your goal, not getting answers about what to do.

♦ Use your intuition and feelings to evaluate the information. How does the entity feel to you intuitively? How does the channel feel to you intuitively? Does the information feel right? How do you feel during the session? Do you feel elated, joyful, uplifted? Or do you feel fearful, dominated, scolded, patronized, flattered, or uncomfortable in any way? If the latter is true, you may be in contact with a low level entity. If this happens, you will want to disregard the information. Always trust yourself. That also will be the message of high level beings.

♦ Don't expect to receive specifics about your soul's plan. The specifics are for you to choose. There are many ways to fulfill your plan, not just a few. You will not receive any information about your plan that might interfere with your unfolding it according to your free will.

Channeling Defined

It might be helpful for you to know something about channeling itself, not only to prepare you for a session with a channel but because some of you may be developing this ability or want to develop it yourself.

Channeling is different from receiving intuitive impressions, although the distinction is not always so clear when this ability is first developing. Channeling, formerly known as mediumship and also known as clairaudience, is the process of receiving communication from nonphysical entities residing in other planes or dimensions. This communication comes in the form of words. The channel is either unconscious, as in classic mediumship, or conscious, as is more common today.

In unconscious channeling, which today is usually called trance channeling rather than mediumship, the channel leaves his or her body temporarily, as it does in sleep, while the entity uses the body, particularly the voice, to convey its message. Afterwards, the medium has no memory of the communication, although he or she may recall traveling to other dimensions or watching the proceedings.

In conscious channeling, the channel is in a light trance, or meditative state, and allows the entity's energy to use the vocal chords and other parts of the body to convey the message. While this is occurring, the channel listens and remains in control of his or her body, and free to interrupt or stop any time. The channel has a sensation of the presence of another energy overlapping his or hers. Conscious channels also receive messages in their minds, which they can then transcribe or convey verbally to others. In this form of channeling, the channel's body is not used, and the messages are received somewhat like thoughts are received.

Whether a channel is conscious or not when channeling is less important than the level of intelligence he or she is able to contact. The more advanced or developed the channel, the higher the level of entity he or she can communicate with. Some channels are not able to reach the higher astral plane and beyond, where higher level entities, including spirit guides, reside. Spirit guides act like guardian angels for each of us, so they are usually the ones who channels try to contact.

Generally, you are better off with a channel who channels

entities from the higher astral plane or beyond rather than one who channels lower astral entities—people awaiting reincarnation. Lower astral entities are not necessarily in a position to offer useful information or guidance, although they will try. Spirit guides and beyond, on the other hand, have finished with their incarnations on earth and its lessons. Therefore, they are much better suited to give guidance and more capable of reading the ethers, where information is recorded.

Below are some questions you might want to ask a channel.

Questions to Ask a Channel

1. How can I improve my relationship with _____?
2. What can you tell me about my life task?
3. How can I further my spiritual progress?
4. What do I need to work on? What is standing in the way of my spiritual progress?
5. How can I find more peace and contentment?
6. Is there an an area of the country that is especially beneficial to me?
7. How can I improve my health?
8. What do I need to do to be more prosperous?
9. What suggestions do you have for making my lifestyle more healthy?
10. What can you tell me about my relationship with _____ that would help me understand it better?
11. Do I have any past-life issues that I need to be more aware of and heal?
12. What healing modality would be most useful for me now in healing my _____?
13. What nutritional suggestions do you have for me?
14. What kind of work am I best suited for?
15. What suggestions do you have for my problem with _____?
16. How might I improve my meditation?
17. How can I best serve others? What kind of service am I best suited for?
18. What are my lessons?
19. Have I known _____ in a previous lifetime? What purpose is this relationship serving?

Notice that none of these questions asks when. Questions about timing are best avoided. They fall into the category of prediction, since timing is rarely set much ahead of time. Even if the timing of something could be known, it is not necessarily for us to know. There are many things that entities know that may not be appropriate for us to know.

High level entities know what information can safely be given to someone and what cannot. They know what might interfere with someone's plan or infringe on free will. They will not give any information that will prevent someone from choosing his or her own course of action. They may encourage a general direction, but never a specific choice. On the other hand, low level entities and psychics who do not know better may give inappropriate information and tell people what they should or should not do. This can be avoided by not asking questions that call for specific advice and by heeding specific advice only when it rings true.

How Channeling and Psychic Abilities Develop

Many of you reading this may have at least the beginnings of the ability to channel. So, some of you may be able to receive some guidance for yourselves not only intuitively but in words. When channeling first develops, isolated words are heard, followed by phrases, sentences, and then paragraphs and more. However, since it takes lifetimes to fully develop the ability to channel, a person might remain at the stage of isolated words for an entire lifetime.

On the other hand, some people regain their ability to channel, developed in previous lifetimes, quite suddenly. Many have no experience of being able to channel until a certain point in their lifetime when they regain this ability. In fact, relatively few channels and psychics have their gifts available to them at birth. When their gifts do appear, they either appear suddenly, as developed as they had been in the past, or are regained gradually over a period of years.

If you have questions about your own channeling or psychic ability, this is something you can ask a channel about. A good channel can give you information about your development, what to do to support it, and how to best use it. Although not everyone will be developed enough to channel for others or even want to, many who have some ability can use it for their own benefit.

Some cautions about development are in order, however. Some people run into problems when they are developing. One's ability to contact higher levels of intelligence is inconsistent during the initial phases of development and even when a channel is regaining a fully developed gift. Because of this, the information he or she receives may be unreliable or, worse, misleading and deceitful. Until a channel has reached a certain level of development, he or she is likely to be in contact with lower astral entities (people who have passed over and are awaiting reincarnation, who may or may not be helpful) more than higher astral entities (spirit guides and teachers). This would not be such a problem if telling who is who was easy, but this can be difficult.

If you have played with a Ouija board, you may have discovered how easy it is to be fooled by lower astral entities. Most of the spirits contacted by ordinary people through Ouija boards are discontent with their state and trying to remain connected to earth through the Ouija board. Some of them fashion themselves as guides, but they are not very good ones. The worst ones to contact are those least evolved, who get their kicks out of deceiving and trying to control people. They impersonate guides, intentionally give false information, and lead people on wild goose chases. Because they sometimes can tell people things an ordinary human being would not know, people often think they are in contact with a real guide. But most of these spirits are not motivated to guide you. Their motives range from having fun to satisfying their own loneliness and longing for the earth plane.

Automatic writing also can present problems for beginning channels. Automatic writing occurs when a nonphysical entity takes control over the arm, hands, and fingers of someone to communicate a message through writing or typing. This is not an uncommon experience for someone who is just developing the ability to channel. When this is occurring, the individual often has no knowledge of what is being written until afterwards when it is read, although some hear the words while they are being written or have an intuitive sense of them. The writing may lack spacing, capitalization, and punctuation, making deciphering it somewhat difficult.

Ouija boards and automatic writing can be a problem, because they enable beginning channels and people who ordinarily would not be able to channel to communicate with those on the astral plane. This would not be a problem if they were assured of contacting those other than lower astral entities. However, without sufficient development, those who use Ouija boards or engage in automatic writing will not be able to reach beyond the lower astral plane consistently. Developed channels, on the other hand, can contact spirit guides and teachers with these props reliably; but they don't need them in the first place.

If you are getting just words or phrases, which will most likely occur when you are meditating or deeply relaxed, you need to be very discriminating. You could consider this a time for learning discernment, a necessary stage for all channels. At this stage, don't expect all communications to be accurate or useful. This will not be true for everyone at this stage, but it is true for enough that it bears some warning. Even when you begin to get more information, you will have to be diligent. If you have any issues at all around discernment or giving your power away, you will be confronted with these lessons during your development.

There is always a temptation to listen to a source outside ourselves before listening to ourselves. How wonderful it would be, many of us feel, to have someone else tell us what to do, where to go, when to do it, and what is going to happen. But that is not what channeling is about. If you are using it that way, you will learn otherwise in your contact with these planes. Channeling, like any gift, is for service to others and to one's own growth. If you are beginning to channel, it is good to ask yourself why you want to channel and what role you want it to play in your life. Examining your motives may help you grow past the difficult lessons that accompany development.

Psychics also have many lessons to learn in their development. Usually their development starts with receiving images, prophetic dreams, bodily sensations, and flashes of knowing. Many also begin seeing spirits and auras, which may happen suddenly or develop over time. When these things first happen, the person does not necessarily understand their meaning, what purpose they serve, or what to do about them. What developing psychics must learn, and often on their own, is how to interpret what they are seeing and feeling, and how to use it to serve others. As you can imagine, there is a big difference between telling someone what you see and using that vision to help that person. It can take lifetimes of psychic development before someone is able to interpret their visions and put them to good use.

Like channeling, some psychics have developed their ability in other lives and are regaining or have regained it, while others are just developing it. If you are developing psychically, asking another psychic or channel about your development is about the only way to get help with this, besides through your own inner guidance. Be sure the person you ask is developed enough to help you.

CHAPTER 7 SUGGESTED READING

About Channeling

Andrews, Lily. *A Guide to Channeling and Channeled Material.* San Rafael, Calif.: Cassandra Press, 1990.

Belhayes, Iris. *Spirit Guides: We Are Not Alone.* San Diego: ACS Publications, 1986

Garfield, Laeh M. and Jack Grant. *Companions in Spirit: A Guide to Working with Your Spirit Helpers.* Berkeley, Calif.: Celestial Arts, 1984.

Klimo, Jon. *Channeling: Investigations on Receiving Information from Paranormal Sources.* Los Angeles: Jeremy P. Tarcher, 1987.

Roman, Sanaya and Duane Packer. *Opening to Channel: How to Connect with Your Guide.* Tiburon, Calif.: H.J. Kramer, 1987.

Channeled Books About the Nature of Reality

Anonymous. *A Course in Miracles.* Tiburon, Calif.: Foundation for Inner Peace, 1975.

Carey, Ken. *The Starseed Transmissions: An Extraterrestrial Report.* Kansas City: UNI-SUN, 1982.

Roberts, Jane. *Seth Speaks.* New York: Bantam Books, 1974.

Rodegast, Pat and Judith Stanton. *Emmanuel's Book: A Manual for Living Comfortably in the Cosmos.* Weston, Conn.: Friends Press, 1985.

Yarbro, Chelsea Quinn. *Messages from Michael.* New York: Playboy Paperbacks, 1979.

Young, Meredith Lady. *Agartha: A Journey to the Stars.* Walpole, N. H.: Stillpoint Publishing, 1984.

Also, books about Edgar Cayce, distributed by A.R.E. and others, are considered classics in the area of metaphysics:

Association for Research and Enlightenment (A.R.E.)
P.O. Box 656
Virginia Beach, VA 23451

CHAPTER 8
Finding Holistic Help

Finding the healing method that is right for you is complicated by a lack of standardized terminology for what alternative healers are doing today. There is no standardized training nor any single method related to terms, such as "transpersonal," "alternative," "holistic," "spiritual," and "New Age," being used to describe the new approaches to emotional and spiritual healing. Although most people understand what psychotherapists do, there are more psychotherapists using nontraditional approaches and more alternative healers without traditional training than ever before. As a result, people looking for help are often left with little guidance or means for evaluating the suitability of an approach for themselves.

The problem of finding good holistic help is magnified by the lack of credentialing and licensing in this area. Esoteric counselors, including astrologers, do not need to be licensed in most places nor do they require any kind of credentials. There are no educational boards or regulators overseeing the activities of many alternative health care practitioners either, such as spiritual healers, aura balancers, energy workers, and crystal healers, although there are schools that provide training and certification in certain techniques. (It's even hard to name these practitioners because of the lack of common language in this area.) Furthermore, new methods are almost as plentiful as practitioners even though the underlying principles of healing in many are the same.

Establishing criteria and licensing for alternative healers and educational institutions will be a major step in transforming the health care system—and in standardizing language in this area—but those days will not come any time soon. Meanwhile, we will have to bear with the inconsistencies, incompetencies, and confusion that come with a new approach to health care. On the following pages are some suggestions to help you through this maze.

Discrimination should also be used once you find a healer or counselor. Abuse of power is always a potential in the healing setting. The therapist/client relationship is inherently unequal, and the client is often in a vulnerable state. However, healers or counselors cannot abuse their power if clients won't let them. Still, it is not the client's responsibility to prevent this. Both are responsible for not falling prey to the temptations of power or dependency.

Guidelines for Selecting a Healer or Esoteric Counselor

♦ Don't use the services of anyone whose credentials or background are questionable. Don't be afraid to ask about previous training and experience. Find out how long they have been practicing, who they have studied with, and what their approach is. Being an informed consumer is as important in this field as in any other. Buyer beware!

♦ Use discrimination in attending psychic fairs. Although some psychic fairs are vehicles for raising the public's awareness of alternative healing methods, the format and name "psychic fair" furthers old stereotypes of gypsy fortunetellers. Readings of a fortunetelling nature foster reliance on outside authorities and are disempowering by implying that the person has nothing to do with his or her future. Alternative healing methods need to create a vehicle other than the psychic fair for demonstrating their methods.

♦ Be wary of anyone who claims to know the future. Any predictions that are made should be given in a tone that acknowledges that the future is fluid, not given as proclamations of certainty. Our future is created in large part by our choices and the choices of those with whom we are involved. These choices can change at any moment, resulting in a future that is in constant flux.

Other influences on our future are our soul's plan and the plans of those with whom we are involved. Although a plan exists, the soul's plan is general, doesn't have to be followed, and rarely has a specific timetable.

♦ Be wary of those who advertise themselves as psychics. People acting as healers rarely call themselves psychics, although they may have psychic gifts. Beware of anyone who claims to have special abilities, especially if he or she flaunts them. Even if they have gifts, their ability to use them well is brought into question by their need to draw attention to them. If you are looking for information like that given by most psychics, you are probably better off going to someone who calls himself or herself a metaphysical or spiritual counselor or something other than a psychic.

(Con'd next page)

♦ Be wary of those who give mostly information that is hard to verify by your own experience or intuition and bears no relevance to your life. Frauds are adept at telling people about their pasts and futures, which are unverifiable. If you receive past-life information, it should relate to current issues. Don't be sidetracked by useless information, even if the information is true. The only reason to go to someone with unusual gifts is to get information that will help you live in harmony with your soul's plan. Those who are not equally motivated to provide information relevant to your growth should be avoided.

♦ Be wary of flattery. Information received from psychics, astrologers, and channels has the potential for being flattering, particularly information about past lives. It is not that all positive information should be suspect, but beware of overly flattering presentations of information. As consumers, we need to question the motives of those who serve us or we run the risk of being taken advantage of.

♦ Let referrals from others guide you in your selection of a healer. If you don't know of anyone who has used the service you are interested in, ask the healer you are considering for references and call those references before making an appointment. Healers with a successful practice will have a loyal following and rely primarily on word of mouth to expand their business. Those who rely heavily on advertising or self-promotion to expand their practice may not be the best. Pay particular attention to how they advertise. Avoid those who make grandiose claims about their abilities or methods.

♦ Be wary of those who claim that no other health care services are needed but theirs. Competent and secure healers recognize the client's complexity and their own fallibility, and frequently make referrals or suggest working concurrently with other professionals. Beware of anyone who is dogmatic or intolerant of other methods.

♦ Interview the person carefully. Find out the person's spiritual orientation and beliefs. Are they compatible with yours?

(Con'd next page)

Also, find out what methods, tools, or approaches he or she uses. Will you be comfortable with them? Will the session be tape-recorded? It should be if it presents information. How do you feel about the person based on your interview? Are you comfortable with him or her on a personality level? These questions are important in determining not only the person's credibility but his or her suitability to your needs.

When esoteric tools are used in the session or the healer is acknowledged as having psychic gifts, it is especially important that the healer act as a facilitator to the client's process and not overpower the client with answers and advice even when asked. Healers should never make choices for clients but, rather, teach them the importance of finding their own answers and making their own choices. Beware if you find a healer telling you what to do or speaking in a tone of voice that implies that he or she is always right. Being discriminating means accepting from the session what is useful and rings true and discarding what does not. Furthermore, you should never come away from a session feeling bad about yourself or frightened; that is a sure sign that something is wrong.

Some of this abuse of power happens because many who go to healers and esoteric counselors expect that someone or some tool knows better than they what they are supposed to do. Actually there is nothing anyone is supposed to do. Some think that because there is a plan, their course is plotted. But the plan is only a general one, with a multitude of potentially fulfilling routes.

Our task—and our responsibility—as individuals is to choose a route. Making choices is at the heart of our evolution: We evolve by making choices and learning from them. When we give up our freedom to do this by allowing others to make choices for us, we inhibit our growth. Likewise, we inhibit our growth when we make choices for someone else, even when asked to.

We also have to be careful not to be taken in by New Age trappings or language. Esoteric tools, New Age accouterments, and even psychic gifts are no assurance that a healer or counselor is on a spiritual path. Spirituality goes beyond psychic phenomena, wearing crystals, or burning incense. We must learn to look beyond these to the sincerity and spiritual dedication of the person.

Ideally, holistic healers and counselors are dedicated to service and their own spiritual growth. They are committed to cultivating their relationship with Spirit through meditation. Asking about someone's spiritual orientation and practices is not too personal when your spiritual well-being is concerned. How can we expect holistic practitioners to heal our souls if they cannot contact their own? This, in the end, is the ultimate touchstone of holistic healers or counselors. The particular tools and methods they use are not nearly as important as their dedication to service and to their own healing and spiritual growth.

The journey toward more effective, holistic healing methods is just begun. Much more needs to unfold, but much is unfolding daily. With a commitment to service and self-transformation by those in this movement and with a greater commitment on our parts to becoming whole, we will see a vast improvement in overall well-being and self-understanding in the future.

CHAPTER 8 SUGGESTED READING

Levine, Frederick G. *The Psychic Sourcebook: How to Choose and Use a Psychic.* New York: Warner Books, 1988.

CONCLUSION

We are discovering that our attitudes and beliefs make a difference in recovering from and avoiding physical illness. Our beliefs are equally important to our emotional well-being. Negative beliefs are often responsible for depression and other negative emotional states. They create negative emotions (and negative outcomes) as assuredly as the announcement "I'm going to work" results in that.

The brain is like a computer that takes commands from us; it does not differentiate between a command that is in our highest good and one that is not. It simply carries out what we affirm. That is the power of affirmation. So, if you affirm "I never succeed no matter what I do," your brain summons the resources of your unconscious to prove this, to manifest this belief. How it does this is beyond our understanding, but metaphysicians have known this and many others accept this intuitively.

To become masters of our own experience, we must use this knowledge consciously to create what we want. I'm not referring so much to manifesting that new car or that new house, but manifesting the lifestyle and the joy we all deserve. What would you like your life to be like, to feel like? What would be necessary to create this? What is stopping you from creating or having this?

If you ask yourself these questions, you may find that you hold certain beliefs that keep you from making the choices that would create what you want. These choices may entail a certain amount of risk, and your beliefs stop you from taking these risks. You may fear losing something or failing in your attempts at creating what you want, so you stay with what you have.

Or sometimes it is our inability to maintain the belief in our dream over a long enough period of time that sabotages it. We give up too soon—we expect too much too soon. Or we don't believe we are worthy of having what we want. The slowness of the manifestation process may tempt us to conclude that we will never have what we want no matter what we do. Some of us conclude this after one year of trying to manifest our dream; some after fifteen years. But the manifestation process will take however long it will take, and our faith and actions must continue until then. Our beliefs are what sustain us through this process.

What has this to do with healing? It may not be obvious, but our ability to manifest what we want has a great deal to do with emotional health and well-being. Negative beliefs and emotions not only prevent us from pursuing our dreams or sabotage them once we have them, but they are what result when we do not achieve what we want.

There are many reasons for not achieving what we want, besides our negative beliefs, including the possibility that we did not work hard enough or skillfully enough or patiently enough to manifest them. Nevertheless, there are times in our lives when we have worked hard, skillfully, and patiently and our desires still do not manifest. When this happens, it may be that what we are trying to manifest is not in keeping with our soul's plan, or it may be that the soul is trying to teach us something by withholding our desires. For instance, we may learn perseverance and patience by not having our efforts rewarded in the usual amount of time.

When we find ourselves frustrated and unable to have what we want, we need to ask: Why is this happening? What possible spiritual purpose could this be serving? Am I trying to manifest something that is contrary to my soul's plan? These are difficult questions to answer. Sometimes we don't find an answer. Still, the act of asking these questions opens us up to receiving spiritual guidance about our situation. This guidance may come to us through our intuition, a dream, the words of a friend or counselor, a book, or any number of ways by which Spirit communicates. When we ask for help in understanding something, we will receive it. Prayer is that powerful.

When we ask for help of this nature, we are asking for a healing. We are asking to heal the disparity between our ego's perception of our situation and our soul's understanding of it. Healing occurs when we align our ego's desires with our soul's. Healing can come either from surrendering to the lesson our soul is trying to teach us by blocking our desires or from reexamining the suitability of our past choices to our spiritual well-being.

When we find ourselves in a negative emotional state, one of three things may be happening:

♦ We may be denying a certain spiritual need, something integral to our spiritual plan. This may be something quite simple, such as ignoring our need for leadership or creativity. Our spiritual needs are described in our astrological chart; they are related and often identical to our psychological needs. When they are not met, we feel depressed, sad, unfulfilled.

♦ We may be learning a painful life lesson, usually for the purpose of developing a virtue such as patience, responsibility, compassion, humility, discernment, or flexibility, to name a few. In this case, we can pray for help in learning the lesson gracefully.

♦ We may have created this negative emotional state by our beliefs or attitudes and are consequently blocking the good that is our due, the good that our soul is trying to manifest for us. This will require that we examine and eliminate the negative beliefs responsible for our pain. Visualizations and affirmations are two tools that can help.

Thus, a complex relationship exists between health—or wholeness—and our thoughts: Our thoughts create emotions that either drive or block our actions. These actions may be in keeping with our soul's plan or not. When our thoughts either block our soul's plan or create something incompatible with it, a negative emotional state results, which must be healed.

Through psychotherapy, we can learn to overcome any negative beliefs that block our actions, but if the actions that result are not in alignment with our soul's plan, we still won't feel whole. So, learning to manage our thoughts and feelings is not enough if we do not know in what direction to apply our will. What direction will be spiritually fulfilling? We need to know whether to continue to pursue our current direction or change it. Are our current difficulties a challenge we must endure and learn from or a message that we must change our course? A holistic approach to feelings tries to answer these questions.

In a holistic approach, the action that is taken next depends on the answer to these questions. Sometimes healing is just a matter of surrendering to what is, to accepting the situation and letting the struggle evolve us. On the other hand, healing may require making new, radical choices. Holistic healing considers each possibility. Its questions assume there is a spiritual plan, a general direction, with which to align. This is a major difference between holistic healing and more traditional methods, which may be satisfied with removing inhibitions to a goal without questioning the value of the goal to the person's spiritual well-being. In holistic healing, understanding the soul's plan is an essential part of healing.

Herein lies the value of meditation. It brings us in contact with our own inner guidance, allowing us to align with our plan and be our own healer. It also opens us to the Light, which ever-awaits our receptivity and is ever-available for our healing. Meditation and its healing Light are our most potent tools for happiness, self-discovery, and self-healing—and they are free for the asking! So ask!

In closing, I'd like to share with you a prayer which was written by Paramahansa Yogananda . May it reverberate in all our hearts:

Heavenly Father, Divine Mother, saints and sages of all religions:

I bow to you all. Lead me to the shores of eternal wisdom and bliss. May Thy love shine forever on the sanctuary of my devotion, and may I be able to awaken Thy love in all hearts. Be Thou the only king reigning on the throne of my consciousness.

O eternal energy, awaken within me conscious will, conscious vitality, conscious health, conscious realization, good will to all, good health to all, vitality to all, realization to all. Eternal youth of body and mind abide within me forever, forever, and forever. Om . . . Peace . . . Bliss . . . Amen.

(Reprinted with permission from the Self-Realization Fellowship.)

To order the following titles, please call **1-800-762-6595**

Nutritious Food with an International Flair.

VEGETARIAN FOOD FOR ALL
Zesty International Dishes from England's
Celebrated Natural Foods Restaurant
By Annabel Perkins
$12.00 192pp.

Inspired by the famous *Food for All* restaurant in Liverpool, England, this collection of tasty international vegetarian recipes offers simple and nutritious food with a creative flair. Each day at the restaurant, the faithful clientele used to arrive with pleasant anticipation, never knowing what marvelous surprises (French, Italian, Mexican, Chinese, Indian, Greek, African?) the author, Annabel Perkins, would serve them. The most mouth-watering results of those culinary experiments have been preserved in this unique cookbook. The recipes are fast and simple enough to be easily prepared from day to day, flexible enough to change with the seasons and to allow scope for your own tastes and creativity.

Includes a wealth of information on foods and kitchen skills.

THE ETHICS OF LOVE
Using Yoga's Timeless Wisdom to Heal Yourself, Your Family and the Earth

Vimala McClure
New Expanded Edition!
$10.00 176 pp.

The Ethics of Love
Using Yoga's Timeless Wisdom to Heal Yourself, Your Family and the Earth

Paranjali's Yoga Sutras for Today's Family
by the Author of *The Tao of Motherhood*

Vimala McClure

New Expanded Edition!

With warmth and deep insight, *The Ethics of Love* explores:

• Non-violent conflict resolution in our families and communities
• Raising children with integrity
• Animal welfare
• Environmental ethics
• The ethics of life & death: abortion, euthanasia, assisted suicide
• Racism, sexism, cultural boundaries
• Communication & conflict management in marriage and partnership
• The economics of simplicity
• Nurturing altruism in our children
• A mission in life: how to set goals and live our soul's plan

The author of bestsellers *Infant Massage: A Handbook for Loving Parents* and *The Tao of Motherhood* takes the teachings of Patanjali concerning kindness, honesty, responsibility, simplicity, unity, clarity, acceptance, sacrifice, broad-mindedness and spirituality, and applies them to the pressing issues of our lives with her special healing touch.

The best part of this book is the feeling of great kindness and good humor that radiates from the pages. There is no pretension here. This is a lovely book about making peace with yourself and your family.
—Pat Wagner, The Bloomsbury Review